The Artful Cupcake

The Artful Cupcake

Baking & Decorating Delicious Indulgences

Marcianne Miller

LARK BOOKS

A Division of Sterling Publishing Co., Inc.
New York

To my sweetie, Lonnie

Art Director
Susan McBride

Photography
Sandra Stambaugh

Cover Design
Barbara Zaretsky

Assistant Editor
Nathalie Mornu

Associate Art Director
Shannon Yokeley

Art Intern
Avery Johnson

Editorial Assistance
Delores Gosnell
Anne Wolff Hollyfield

Library of Congress Cataloging-in-Publication Data

Miller, Marcianne.
  The artful cupcake : baking & decorating delicious indulgences /
Marcianne Miller.
     p. cm.
Includes index.
  ISBN 1-57990-461-0
  1. Cake decorating. I. Title.
  TX771.2.M55 2004
  641.8'653--dc21

10 9 8 7 6

Published by Lark Books, a division of
Sterling Publishing Co., Inc.
387 Park Avenue South, New York, N.Y. 10016

© 2004, Lark Books

Distributed in Canada by Sterling Publishing,
c/o Canadian Manda Group, 165 Dufferin Street
Toronto, Ontario, Canada M6K 3H6

Distributed in the United Kingdom by GMC Distribution Services,
Castle Place, 166 High Street, Lewes, East Sussex, England BN7 1XU

Distributed in Australia by Capricorn Link (Australia) Pty Ltd.,
P.O. Box 704, Windsor, NSW 2756 Australia

If you have questions or comments about this book, please contact:
Lark Books
67 Broadway
Asheville, NC 28801
(828) 253-0467
Manufactured in China

ISBN 13: 978-1-57990-461-6
ISBN 10: 1-57990-461-0

For information about custom editions, special sales, premium and corporate
purchases, please contact Sterling Special Sales Department at 800-805-5489
or specialsales@sterlingpub.com.

Contents

Introduction

Eating a cupcake is a simple childlike delight, like finding a treasure placed in the palm of your hand. And no matter how artful and grown-up we make a cupcake, in creating it, we tap the passion for color, shape, texture, and sweet-tasting things in which we once took such unabashed pleasure.

A cupcake is not plain like a pound cake or flat like a pancake. It's a two-story affair, a cake base crowned with a yummy topping, which in turn is often adorned with sugar confections of every conceivable size and shape. Though the cake parts are usually variations on themes of white, yellow, and chocolate, their embellishments are taken from every color in the artist's palette and a seemingly endless range of flavors from the pantry.

You can eat a cupcake with a fork if all the people around you seem to be on their best behavior. But when no one's looking, you can just pick it up and wolf it down in about seven bites. (Notice that precise count!) A cupcake is unlike a layered cake or a pie that you have to be nice and slice up portions for someone else. When you see a cupcake resting on a plate or nestled in a basket, you know you can say to yourself, *It's mine, all mine!*

At the same time, no one ever makes just one cupcake. Whether it's for a school event, a business meeting, a dinner party, a community fundraiser, or for the guys coming over to watch football, we make cupcakes with the intention of sharing them with others. The ultimate joy of cupcakes is that you get to eat all your cake and keep your friends happy, too.

We defined a cupcake as an individual cake that spent some part of its creation in a muffin pan. An artful cupcake is one that has been baked and decorated in a skillful manner, with a deliberate attempt to make it beautiful. The elements of such a cupcake—the cake, its topping, the decorations, the way it's presented—are planned and arranged in a harmonious relationship. An artful cupcake must also taste as good as it looks.

Cupcakes are small cakes.

Unless they're like a pie...

or a cookie...

or custard...

or cheesecake ...

or beyond description.

Twelve professional bakers designed and created the 36 cupcake projects for this book, so you'll see a wide variety of recipes, decorating techniques, and special tools.

Modified for the home baker, these projects are relatively easy to make, using ingredients that are readily available. Since many dessert makers learn to bake with cupcakes, we've filled the pages with tips for the beginning baker, and included lots of creative challenges for the experienced baker, too.

From one cupcake lover to another, may you have as much fun making the cupcakes in this book as we did. May you delight your family, impress your friends, and sell more homemade goodies at the neighborhood bake sale than anybody else. And may you have as much difficulty as we did deciding which cupcake was our favorite—the only way to do that, of course, is to sample each one.

Enjoy!

7

Most cupcakes are round.   Unless they're squares...   or triangles...   or hearts...   or starbursts.

The Basics of Making Artful Cupcakes

To make artful cupcakes, you apply the same guiding principles you follow in your other creative pursuits. Use the best materials and tools. Set up and maintain an organized working space. Follow the advice of experts until you're experienced yourself. Practice, practice. Proudly show off your creations so everyone can enjoy them.

USE THE BEST INGREDIENTS

In baking terms, best means fresh—the freshest dairy products of whole milk, cream (usually heavy), unsalted butter, and large eggs; fresh dry ingredients including flour, baking soda, baking powder, and cornstarch; plump, juicy fruits; crunchy nuts; good wine; aromatic spices; and top quality chocolate.

Fresh ingredients are the basis of delicious homemade cupcakes.

Bring Ingredients to Room Temperature

All ingredients should be at room temperature, unless specified differently. When you're planning to bake, the first thing you should do is remove your refrigerated ingredients so they have at least an hour (more if the room is cool) to warm up.

About Butter

Butter should be softened, that is, malleable and easy to cut. To hasten the process, slice each stick into eight portions. Don't heat butter in the microwave because what usually happens is a mess: the middle melts and the sides stay cool. Here's a safe compromise: give the butter an initial warming boost in the microwave with 2 minutes at the lowest setting, remove it, and let it finish warming up on its own.

Our recipes usually indicate the ounces of butter required and the equivalent number of sticks. Many recipes, especially those passed down in families, indicate butter in

Butter Equivalents

2 oz = ½ stick (or 4 tablespoons or ¼ cup or ⅛ pound)

4 oz = 1 stick (8 tablespoons or ½ cup or ¼ pound)

8 oz = 2 sticks (1or 6 tablespoons or 1 cup or ½ pound)

cups or pounds. See the handy chart above to help you bring those old-fashioned treats to today's table.

Can you use whipped or tub butter? No, the whipping process affects the way the butter mixes with other ingredients. Can you use margarine instead of butter in the recipes? Yes, but do remember the taste will not be as luscious.

If you want to use low-fat butters and margarines, choose brands that have at least 5 to 6 grams of fat. Anything less doesn't work well in baking. Also, the substitution is not equal amounts. The low-fat versions are diluted with water, so

you need use only three-fourths as much of them as you would the standard full-fat forms.

About Flour

Most cupcake recipes call for wheat flour, either all-purpose flour or cake flour, which is refined and bleached. Use the type of flour specified. If a recipe requires sifted flour, you should indeed sift it because it makes a difference in how the cake turns out. Otherwise, scoop the flour into a measuring cup and smooth it with a spatula.

About Wheat Flour Substitutions

A growing number of people are on special diets that don't include wheat. This doesn't mean they have to say good-bye to cupcakes, for there are many tasty substitutions for wheat. (The gluten-free Poppyseed & Almond Cupcakes recipe on page 78 uses potato starch.) In general, for each cup of wheat flour in a recipe, you can make one of the following substitutions:

- 1 cup corn flour
- ⅝ cup potato starch flour
- ⅞ cup rice flour (brown or white, depending on the color you want)
- ½ cup ground seeds or nuts

CHOOSE GOOD EQUIPMENT AND BAKEWARE

Your baking dollars are wisely spent on equipment and bakeware that will stand the test of time. Do comparison shop, but in general, buy the best you can afford. Choose glass or stainless steel instead of plastic, buy tried and true brands instead of less expensive imitations. Quality always counts, whether it's the brushes you paint with or the pans for your baking.

Cupcake baking requires the same equipment you probably already have on hand for making cakes, pies, cookies, candy, and other sweet treats.

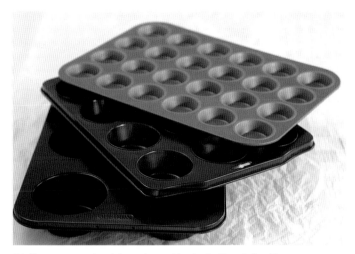

Muffin pans come in mini, regular, and jumbo (or Texas) size. If you use nonstick pans, be sure to reduce baking temperature or time.

Silicone muffin pans are convenient and a dream to clean. A high-quality baking sheet and wire cooling rack are necessary.

With new bakeware, such as this nonstick bundt pan, you can make three different cupcake shapes at the same time. Incredible!

Cupcake equipment includes all of the traditional baking standbys—a mixer with a paddle attachment if you have one, a handheld mixer if you don't; and the usual assortment of wooden spoons, measuring cups and spoons, a set of mixing bowls, a sifter, a sieve, a rolling pin, and a candy thermometer. Newer items you might consider putting on your gift list are silicone mats, which won't let anything stick to their surface, and graters with easy-grip handles. Essentials include a sharp serrated knife and a cupcake size frosting spatula.

Experienced bakers are meticulous about keeping their tools clean and wiping them off constantly between different uses. Remember to sterilize small tools like tweezers that you use to place tiny decorations or hold fragile flowers.

Most recipes are still written for traditional medium-weight shiny metal muffin pans. If you use the nonstick pans, remember the dark metal will brown the edges faster, so lower the baking temperature by 25°F or decrease the baking time. The newer silicone muffin pans require no greasing and offer an exciting variety of cup shapes, including pyramids and squares. Because they're so bendable, they need to be placed on a baking sheet before going into the oven.

Spray cooling racks with nonstick spray to keep cakes from sticking and to reduce cleanup time. Place the racks over parchment paper or a baking sheet to catch drips from decorating with chocolate, fruit glazes, and sanding sugars.

11

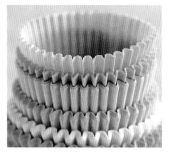

To keep pastel paper cups from looking washed out, bake cupcakes in two nestled baking cups.

For special occasions, use shiny foil baking cups.

To show off attractive cake and create smooth sides, bake cupcakes without baking cups.

MAKE THE BOTTOMS PRETTY

Traditionally cupcakes have been baked in fluted baking cups, paper or foil. The cups keep cakes fresh and give a distinctive pattern to their sides. They come in a wide range of colors and in all three sizes, so you'll never be at a loss for pretty cupcake bottoms.

When you want the sides of the cake to be smooth, don't use a baking cup. Unless you're using the silicone pans, grease the muffin pans, even the nonstick ones. Though some bakers swear by greasing with butter, others think it browns the sides of the cake too much and prefer vegetable shortening or cooking oil spray. A non-stick spray made especially for baking combines an oil spray with flour—it's the ideal way to grease a muffin pan, so keep your eyes open for it.

Vintage china saucers create charming cupcake arrangements.

DISPLAY CUPCAKES IN STYLE

With their small shapes and playful demeanor, cupcakes are natural show-offs. Sitting atop a cake plate or peeking out of a basket, alone or with a baker's dozen, they always look ready to be picked up and eaten. Decorate display plates with colored sugars, shaved chocolate, chopped nuts, flower petals, and strings of shiny beads. Transform an ordinary baking sheet into a splendid serving tray by draping it with pretty cloth napkins or fitting it with aluminum foil topped with sugar and candies.

Contemporary cupcake displays are perfect for gala events.

CUPCAKE
BAKING BASICS

In cooking, you can add a bit of this, a tad of that, and often come out with a dish that is appetizing. Baking is much more scientific. The method and the sequence in which you combine ingredients, the oven temperature and baking time, even how humid the weather is can have an effect on baking and decorating. You can improve your chances of success if you follow a few baking fundamentals.

Follow the Directions

Unless you're an experienced baker, follow the directions given for each project. Information on how to decorate the project is indicated first, listing the "materials" you'll need (such as completed recipes, specific decorating ingredients, and any special tools), followed by the numbered steps of the decorating process. The instructions vary from a few sentences to several paragraphs, depending on how complex the project is. The accompanying photos are highlights of the decorating steps, presented in their general sequence.

Each project includes a recipe. It can be an original recipe specific to the project, or one of the basic cupcake recipes on pages 18 and 19. Each recipe indicates how many cupcakes it will yield, generally in multiples of 12, since that's the number of cupcakes in the standard muffin pan.

Recipe amounts are given in U.S. measurements. Metric conversions and handy measurement equivalents are in the back of the book on page 140.

The recipes were designed specifically for cupcakes, which means the suggested baking time has been adjusted for their smaller size. If you use cake recipes from other sources, be sure to reduce the baking time 15 or 20 minutes.

Most cake recipes (except sponge cakes, which need plenty of room to rise) convert easily to cupcakes:

Cake Recipe	Regular Cupcakes
One 8-inch square cake =	12 cupcakes
One 9 x 13-inch cake =	18 cupcakes
Two 9-inch round layers =	24 cupcakes
Two 8-inch round layers =	18 cupcakes

For some glamorous projects—such as the Chocolate Mousse Layered Cake on page 80—we assume you'll decorate only a few cupcakes at any one time. In those cases, bake all the batter the recipe calls for, use the number of cupcakes you need for that project, and reserve the rest for another project. Most cupcakes refrigerate and freeze well, so you won't have to lose any cupcakes. (See Storing Cupcakes on page 17.)

Fill Muffin Cups Properly

To give the cakes room to rise, fill each muffin cup about two-thirds full, or less, if the recipe indicates. If you have too much batter, fill as many muffin cups as you can, let them cool, then bake another batch. If you have too little batter, fill the empty cups two-thirds full with water to even out the pan.

Use Your Oven Properly

Of course, you always need to preheat the oven before you set the cupcakes inside. It usually takes about 15 to 20 minutes for an average-size oven to reach baking temperature. Few ovens are accurate, and the temperature in most is not steady throughout the baking process, so the best way to get consistent results is to bake in the center of the oven and center the baking pan on the rack.

Check for Doneness

Recipes give a range of time for baking, say 15 to 20 minutes. Check after the initial time has elapsed to see if the cakes are done. The best way to do this is the old-fashioned method—stick a toothpick into the center of one cupcake. If it comes out clean, meaning with no raw batter on it, the cake is done.

Cool Cupcakes Before Cutting and Frosting

Unless a recipe indicates otherwise, always allow your cupcakes to cool before you cut or decorate them. The best way to do this is to set them on a wire cooling rack and leave them alone for a half-hour.

Use a sharp, serrated knife to cut a cupcake into layers, or to flatten its top to hold a glaze. Hold the cupcake firmly in one hand, keeping fingers away from the path of the knife, and cut the cake with a steady, horizontal slice.

DECORATING CUPCAKES

There are as many ways to decorate cupcakes as there are to combine ingredients to bake them. In the following pages, you'll discover a marvelous variety of decorating techniques, from traditional frosting to elegant fruit glazes, from snow-white meringue to wonderfully wicked chocolate ganache. But never let it be said that we leave frosting well enough alone. A bed of buttercream is meant to be embellished—that's why we love candies and colored sugars, and turn our creative ways to making edible art like white chocolate roses painted with petal dust.

Frosting and Icing

Frosting is that fluffy, sugary indulgence we feel compelled to taste before it's finished, the one most associated with our cupcake memories. Three traditional frosting recipes are on pages 18 and 19, including two versions of basic buttercream frosting. Once you know how to make it, you can flavor buttercream frosting with extracts and juices and give it any color of the rainbow.

Icing refers to the thinner toppings such as traditional Royal Icing, and the unfussy water icing.

With some frostings you can't seem to stop using that spatula!

This dainty cupcake is a combination of two icings: water icing covers the cupcake and Royal Icing makes the flowers.

Shaping Frosting

Some people, remembering ceiling-high wedding cakes, get a glazed look in their eyes when they hear the phrase "cupcake decorating." We figure they're just folks who haven't yet learned the pleasure of using a decorating pastry bag. Sculpting and shaping frosting is so enjoyable that once you learn how to do it, you'll wonder why you ever bored yourself with store-bought cupcakes.

The tip you place on the end of the pastry bag shapes the frosting as you squeeze it out.

There is a galaxy of metal decorating tips with different shapes, but in the beginning you can do fine with a few tips, such as the star-shaped tip. Decorating instructions usually indicate which tip you should use. Sometimes, especially in American recipes, only the number of the point is given. This number refers to a point made by Wilton, the major manufacturer of pastry tips.

Pastry decorating tools are minimal: a sturdy, reusable pastry bag with a variety of fitted tips, a small frosting spatula, food coloring, and parchment paper and scissors to make your own pastry bags.

Hold the pastry bag straight up to make some styles of frosting.

On other styles, you'll hold the pastry bag sideways.

Using a Pastry Bag

1. Fit the tip on the end of the bag.

2. Fold back the top edge of the bag to keep it from tipping over and spilling the frosting.

3. Scoop the frosting about halfway into the bag. (You can work with a fuller bag after you've gained some experience.)

4. Hold the bag in your hands and squeeze the frosting in the bag through the tip onto the cake. The directions usually indicate how you should hold the pastry bag so the frosting squeezes through the tip in the shape desired.

5. Unless the directions say otherwise, work from the center out. (You'll make a bunch of buttercream blobs on your first attempts. That's okay, eat your mistakes or scrape them back into the pastry bag and start again.)

Note: We don't recommend using a pastry bag filled with hot ingredients, such as melted chocolate or sugar, until you've gained some experience holding and squeezing the bag.

Coloring Frosting

Color is such an exciting part of cupcake decorating that sometimes all you need to wow the crowd is a simple array of different colored cupcakes. Remember that buttercream usually has a slight ivory cast that affects the resulting color of your dye. Generally, for adults, less color is more attractive, so go lightly with it. Usually a few drops will color a whole cup of frosting.

Other Toppings

In addition to lots of frosting variations, the projects provide a mini-sampler of other cupcake decorating techniques. It's positively amazing the number of ways you can decorate that unassuming little cup of cake and how one technique leads happily to another, and to another...

Paint with petal dust.

Specialty food coloring, found in craft stores and on the Internet, creates the intense color you want for some party displays.

Create snowflakes.

Go crazy with chocolate ganache.

Buttercream frosting takes color beautifully and a drop or two changes its intensity.

Make crystallized flowers.

Be totally sophisticated.

STORING CUPCAKES

Most cupcakes store well. Cool the cakes completely before storing them. Wrap them in heavy-duty foil or plastic wrap, getting out as much air as possible, then place them in airtight, moisture-proof containers such as plastic containers with tight-fitting lids. They'll stay fresh for several days in the refrigerator.

Unfrosted cakes will freeze for up to six months. Let them thaw at room temperature for 2 to 3 hours. If desired, freshen them for 5 minutes in a 350°F oven or in the microwave on low for a few seconds. Then frost them.

Frosted cakes will freeze for up to three months. First place the frosted cakes into the freezer to harden the frosting, remove them to cover them tightly, then return them to the freezer in a container to avoid crushing them. Thaw them gradually, overnight, in the refrigerator.

It's always okay to make lots of frosting so you can spread it thickly if you wish, and then have plenty on hand for another batch of cupcakes. In an airtight container, frosting can stay fresh several days in the refrigerator or up to two months in the freezer.

Meringue frostings and custard-type fillings don't freeze well, so enjoy these shortly after you make them.

WHERE TO BUY CUPCAKE SUPPLIES

Used to running up to the art supply store when we were low on paint or paper, we were surprised to discover that gathering the supplies we wanted for our artful cupcakes was not so easy. In the grocery store, unsalted butter was in a different section from the salted butter; multicolored baking cups were two aisles over from the plain pastel cups. Sparkles were there, but sanding sugars could be found only in a specialty baking store. The search for top quality baking chocolate took us all over town. For this reason, if a recipe calls for an item that's not ordinarily found in a typical grocery store, we indicate in parentheses where you're likely to find it.

If you're new to cupcake decorating and unfamiliar with local suppliers, go on a few scouting expeditions before a big baking day. Your best sources of information are baker friends and neighbors, so get their advice first. Most specialty decorating items are available through mail order catalogs and almost all of them have websites. If you type "cupcake" in your Internet search engine, you'll instantly enter an astonishing universe of cupcake decorating suppliers and ideas. Have fun!

Basic Cupcake Recipes

Classic White Cupcakes

1¾ cups sifted cake flour
2 teaspoons baking powder
¼ teaspoon salt
¾ cup milk
2 teaspoons vanilla extract
1¼ cups sugar
4 oz (1 stick) unsalted butter, room temperature 3 egg whites

1. Preheat the oven to 350°F and prepare the muffin pans with nonstick spray and flour or paper cups.

2. Resift the sifted cake flour with the baking powder and salt.

3. Combine the milk and vanilla.

4. Cream the sugar and butter until fluffy.

5. Alternating the flour mixture with the milk mixture, blend half of one, then the other into the butter mixture. Mix well after each addition and repeat. Mix until well blended.

6. In a separate bowl, beat the egg whites until stiff, but not dry. Fold them into the batter.

7. Pour the batter into the muffin pans, filling at least halfway. Bake for 15 to 20 minutes, until the cakes test done.

8. Remove the pans and turn out the cupcakes onto a wire rack to cool.

Yields 24 cupcakes

Easy Yellow Cupcakes

2¼ cups sifted cake flour

1¼ cups sugar

3 teaspoons baking powder

1 teaspoon salt

½ cup vegetable oil

1 cup milk

2 eggs

2 teaspoons vanilla extract

1. Preheat the oven to 350°F and prepare the muffin pans with nonstick spray and flour or paper cups.

2. In a large bowl, mix together the flour, sugar, baking powder, and salt until thoroughly blended.

3. Whisk together the oil and milk and add to the dry ingredients. Beat for 2 minutes on medium speed.

4. Add the eggs and vanilla and beat again for 2 minutes on medium.

5. Pour the batter into the pans, filling at least halfway. Bake for 15 to 20 minutes, until the cakes test done.

6. Remove the pans and turn out the cupcakes onto a wire rack to cool.

Yields 24 cupcakes

Chocolate Buttermilk Cupcakes

1⅔ cups flour

1 teaspoon baking soda

½ teaspoon salt

½ cup unsweetened cocoa

1 cup sugar

1 cup buttermilk

½ cup vegetable oil

1 teaspoon vanilla extract

1. Preheat the oven to 350°F and prepare the muffin pans with nonstick spray and flour or paper cups.

2. In a large bowl, sift together the flour, baking soda, and salt. Add the cocoa and sugar and mix until thoroughly blended.

3. Add the buttermilk, oil, and vanilla and beat until smooth.

4. Pour or spoon the batter into the pans, filling at least halfway. Bake for 15 to 20 minutes, until the cakes test done.

5. Remove the pans and turn out the cupcakes onto a wire rack to cool.

Yields 24 cupcakes

Basic Frosting Recipes

Classic Buttercream Frosting

6 oz (1½ sticks) unsalted butter, softened

2¼ cups confectioners' sugar

Liquid food coloring (optional)

2 tablespoons milk or fruit juice (optional)

1. Place the softened butter in a large bowl.

2. Gradually add the sugar by sifting a small amount over the butter and stirring to incorporate. Continue until all the sugar is blended in.

3. Beat hard with a wooden spoon or an electric mixer until the icing is pale and fluffy.

4. A small amount of food coloring may be added toward the end of the beating. Bear in mind that the butter gives this icing a pale yellow tint that will affect the resulting color.

5. Beat in the milk or juice, if desired.

Note: If you desire a softer or flavored icing, choose either milk or fruit juice to complement the flavor of the cupcake. The longer the buttercream is beaten, the lighter the texture will become, since beating incorporates air into the mixture. If you want a firmer, bulkier icing, add more sifted confectioners' sugar. You can use up to double the amount of sugar to the amount of butter.

Buttercream can be weather sensitive, reacting to barometric pressure or the rain by breaking up. If that happens, try to salvage it by taking out the cracked part, remixing it, and then recombining it into the remaining frosting. It always helps to have a supply of buttercream frosting on hand for last minute parties. If covered in an airtight container, buttercream frosting can stay safely in the refrigerator for days and up to 2 months in the freezer.

Yields enough for 16 to 24 cupcakes

Ivory Buttercream Frosting

1 lb confectioners' sugar, sifted

4 oz (1 stick) unsalted butter, room temperature

⅛ to ¼ cup whipping cream

1 teaspoon clear vanilla extract

Special Tools

Electric mixer

1. Combine all ingredients, beginning with the smaller portion of whipping cream, in the large bowl of an electric mixer. Mix on low until well blended.

2. Depending on humidity and/or temperature, you may need to add more cream to make the frosting a spreading consistency. Do so a spoonful at a time, beating to incorporate, then test the consistency after each addition.

Note: This recipe calls for "clear vanilla extract," which has no artificial coloring. Using it will make the frosting whiter. It's available at many groceries in the baking section, along with regular vanilla. If it's not readily available, you can use regular vanilla extract.

Recipe by Jane Tomlinson

Yields enough for 12 cupcakes

Cream Cheese Frosting

8 oz cream cheese, room temp

4 oz (1 stick) unsalted butter, softened

1 lb confectioners' sugar, sifted

1 teaspoon vanilla extract

Special Tools

Electric mixer with a paddle attachment

1. In the bowl of the electric mixer, cream together the cream cheese and butter until very smooth and fluffy.

2. Add the confectioners' sugar in three increments, mixing well after each addition.

3. Add the vanilla extract, and mix until smooth.

4. Store, covered, in the refrigerator until ready to use.

Yields enough for 16 to 24 cupcakes

Design and Recipes by Rose Reitzel-Perry

Coconut & Lime Cupcakes

Striking Art Deco colors—coconut white, lime green, and berry black—combine to make an ultra-contemporary cupcake flower that is as delicious as it is distinctive.

Materials

24 Coconut Cupcakes (recipe page 24)

Lime Curd (recipe page 25)

¾ cup wide strips of unsweetened coconut (found in specialty markets)

24 fresh blackberries

Design Tip

This cupcake is equally delicious with lemon curd, which you can often find premade in grocery stores.

Instructions

1. Spread the cooled lime curd on top of the cooled cupcakes.

2. Insert the coconut flakes sideways into the curd on top of each cake. Like petals, place them in overlapping concentric circles, starting from just above the top of the baking cup and working upward.

3. Top each "flower" with a blackberry.

Coconut Cupcakes

Note: The coconut milk used in this recipe is unsweetened and can be found with Thai foods in grocery stores. The coconut milk that you find with drink mixes has been sweetened.

¾ cup wide strips of unsweetened coconut
(found in specialty markets)

1¼ cups unsweetened coconut milk

1 egg

3 egg whites

2¾ cups cake flour

1 tablespoon baking powder

½ teaspoon salt

8 oz (2 sticks) unsalted butter,
room temperature

1½ cups sugar

1. Preheat the oven to 350°F. Prepare the muffin pans with nonstick spray. If you want the cupcakes to have smooth sides, don't use baking cups.

2. Soak the coconut strips in ¼ cup of the coconut milk. Set aside.

3. Combine the remaining cup of coconut milk with the egg and egg whites.

4. Sift together the flour, baking powder, and salt.

5. Cream the butter and sugar together until pale and fluffy. Add the soaked coconut flakes.

6. Add the egg mixture to the butter mixture in three parts, alternating with the flour mixture in two parts. Between additions, mix thoroughly and scrape down the sides of the bowl.

7. Pour the batter into the prepared pans, filling approximately halfway. Bake 18 to 20 minutes, until the tops are starting to color.

8. Let the cupcakes rest a couple of minutes in the pans, then turn them out onto a cooling rack and allow them to cool completely before icing.

Lime Curd

1 teaspoon water

½ teaspoon unflavored gelatin

4 egg yolks

½ cup sugar

Juice of 3 limes

Green food coloring

Zest of 1 lime

2 oz (½ stick) unsalted butter,
softened and cut into pieces

1. Put the water in a small mixing bowl and sprinkle the gelatin over it to soften.

2. In a heavy saucepan, whisk the egg yolks and sugar to blend thoroughly. Whisk in the lime juice.

3. Place the saucepan on medium heat. Stirring constantly (but not vigorously) with a wooden spoon, cook the mixture until it begins to steam and then thickens. When you can draw a line with your finger across the curd on the back of the stirring spoon and the line stays without dripping, take it off the heat.

4. Strain the curd into the mixing bowl with the gelatin, and whisk to incorporate.

5. Put a drop of green food coloring in a small dish, and use a toothpick to transfer just a smidgen to the mixture (a full drop might make the mixture too dark). Stir to see the effect. Continue until you reach the desired pale green.

6. Add the zest and butter, and whisk until the butter is melted and everything is an even color.

7. Refrigerate 30 minutes, or until the lime curd has thickened to a spreadable consistency.

Design and Recipe by Martha Vining

Chocolate with Cabernet Cupcakes

It looks like an ordinary chocolate cupcake until you bite into it, and then—my oh my, what an adult-rated surprise it is—super-rich chocolate with the taste of cherries and the slightest hint of red wine.

Materials

18 Chocolate with Cabernet Cupcakes (recipe at right)

2 cups lightly sweetened whipped cream

¼ cup dried cherries, chopped

1 tablespoon cinnamon or cocoa powder as garnish

Instructions

1. Spoon a dollop of whipped cream on the center of the completely cooled cupcakes.

2. Add five to six bits of dried fruit and a dusting of cinnamon or cocoa powder.

Time-Saving Tip

Adults love these cupcakes. So make more than you need for one event and freeze the rest. Stored in an airtight bag, they should keep well up to two months.

Chocolate with Cabernet Cupcakes

1½ cups all-purpose flour

1 cup sugar

1 teaspoon baking soda

½ teaspoon baking powder

1 teaspoon salt

1 teaspoon cinnamon

½ cup unsweetened cocoa powder

½ cup vegetable oil

1 teaspoon vanilla extract

2 eggs

¾ cup cabernet sauvignon wine

½ cup dried cherries, chopped

1. Preheat the oven to 350°F and prepare muffin pans with white paper baking cups.

2. Into the large bowl of an electric mixer, sift together the flour, sugar, baking soda, baking powder, salt, cinnamon, and cocoa powder.

3. Add the oil, vanilla, eggs, and wine.

4. Beat with the electric mixer at low speed for 30 seconds. Turn the mixer speed to high and continue beating for 3 minutes, scraping the sides occasionally.

5. Remove the bowl from the mixer and stir in the dried cherries. Pour the batter into the prepared muffin pans. Bake for 20 minutes or until a toothpick inserted comes out clean.

Yields 6 cupcakes

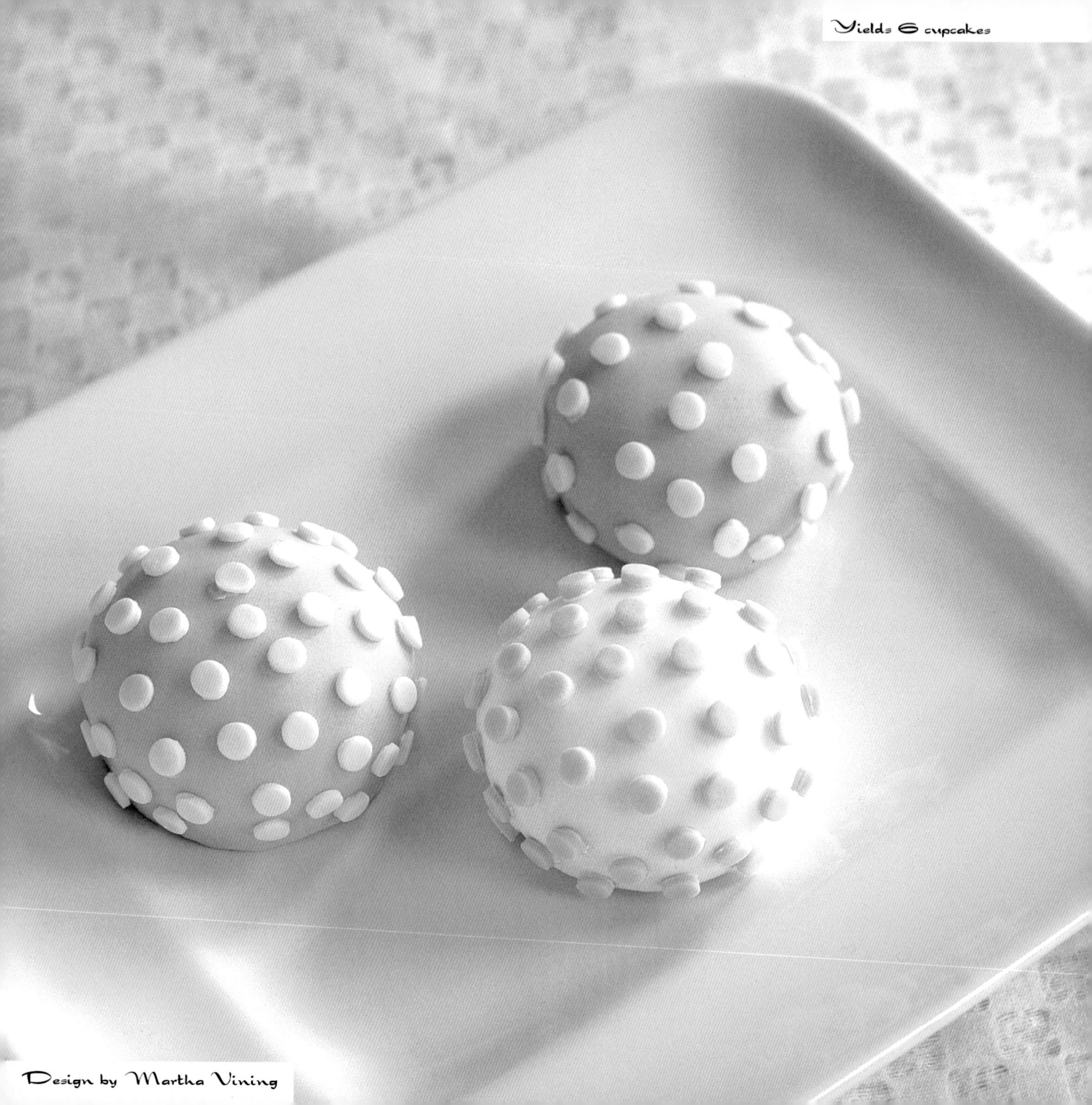

Design by Martha Vining

Polka Dot Fondant Cupcakes

Decorating with fondant is as fun as sculpting with clay. Shape the fondant with your hands to create elegant matte-finish cakes that are right at home with fine china and silver. Then add mischievous touches, such as pop-up polka dots.

Materials

6 Classic White or Easy Yellow Cupcakes (recipes on page 16 or 17)

24 oz (3 cups) rolled Tasty Fondant (recipe on page 130)

1 cup Royal Icing (recipe on page 65)

2 to 3 drops desired food coloring

1 cup confectioners' sugar

¾ cup apricot jam, melted

Special Tools

Rolling pin

Smooth surface, such as a pastry board or marble slab

1-inch pastry brush

Pastry bag with #12 decorating tip

Design Tip

When working with fondant, turn it frequently and dust with confectioners' sugar to prevent it from sticking.

Instructions

1. Take three-quarters of the Tasty Fondant and work in food coloring with your hands until no streaks are visible. Keep all the rolled fondant wrapped tightly in plastic and the remainder in an airtight container to prevent it from drying until you are ready to use.

2. Divide the remaining colored fondant into six equal portions, approximately ⅔ cup each. Using a rolling pin on a smooth surface, roll it into a 6-inch circle, approximately ¼ inch thick. (Because you want a perfectly smooth finish to the fondant, don't roll it out on a silicone pastry mat—the textured surface could leave an imprint.)

3. Brush the sides and tops of the cupcakes with melted apricot jam to make the tasty "glue" that will hold the fondant to the cupcake.

4. Drape the fondant circle over a cupcake and shape with clean, dry hands to completely cover the top and sides. Trim around the bottom with a sharp paring knife to form a neat, clean edge.

5. Roll out the remaining uncolored fondant to the same ¼-inch thickness. With the decorating tip, cut out dots about the size of a pencil eraser.

6. Use a toothpick to push each dot through the decorating tip onto the tip of your finger.

7. Dab the dot with a spot of Royal Icing—this will make it adhere to the fondant. Repeat for all the dots and apply them randomly to the fondant in a pleasing array.

8. Allow completed cupcakes to dry 3 to 4 hours, then use a metal spatula to lift them from below and move them to your display plate.

29

Design and Recipes by Linda Brown

Tropical Paradise Cupcakes

One serving of this coconut and fruit delight and you'll think you've escaped to an island paradise—maybe that's why this cupcake is as popular in the middle of winter as it is in summertime!

Materials

24 Coconut & Fruit Cupcakes (recipe page 32)

Cream Cheese & Orange Frosting (recipe at right)

1 cup coconut strips, sweetened or unsweetened

½ cup chopped pecans, toasted or untoasted

Instructions

1. Spread the tops of the cakes with a thick layer of frosting.

2. Press the coconut strips one at a time all over the frosting of each cake, letting some stick out sideways, some stand up straight. The wide unsweetened coconut strips in the cupcake photo have a natural, chewy taste. You can find them in specialty markets.

For the traditional softer and sweeter taste, use the thinner sweetened coconut strips found in the baking section of your grocery store.

3. Press chopped pecans into the frosting between the coconut strips.

Cream Cheese and Orange Frosting

4 oz (1 stick) unsalted butter, room temperature
8 oz cream cheese, room temperature
1 lb confectioners' sugar, sifted
1 teaspoon orange zest
1 teaspoon vanilla extract
½ teaspoon orange extract

1. In the bowl of an electric mixer fitted with a paddle attachment, cream together the butter and cream cheese on medium speed for 5 minutes. Scrape the sides of the bowl with a rubber spatula.

2. On low speed, add the confectioners' sugar in three additions, mixing well between each addition. Scrape the sides of the bowl.

3. Add the orange zest, vanilla, and orange extract. Mix well and store in an airtight container in the refrigerator until ready to use.

Coconut and Fruit Cupcakes

1 cup pecan pieces

3 cups all-purpose flour

1 teaspoon baking powder

½ teaspoon baking soda

½ teaspoon cinnamon

½ teaspoon salt

⅛ teaspoon nutmeg

4 oz (1 stick) unsalted butter, room temperature

2 cups sugar

4 eggs

1 cup milk

1 teaspoon vanilla extract

½ teaspoon orange extract

1 teaspoon orange zest

1 ripe banana, mashed

8 oz pineapple tidbits with juice

1 cup sweetened coconut

1. Preheat the oven to 350°F and prepare muffin pans with white or pastel paper cups.

2. Toast the pecans by putting them on a baking pan in the heated oven for 5 minutes. Set them aside to add later.

3. Sift together the flour, baking powder, baking soda, cinnamon, salt, and nutmeg.

4. In the bowl of an electric mixer fitted with a paddle attachment, cream the butter and sugar at medium speed until light and fluffy. Scrape the sides of the bowl with a rubber spatula.

5. On low speed, add the eggs one at a time, mixing well between each addition.

6. In a separate bowl, combine the milk, vanilla, and orange extract.

7. Add the flour mixture in three additions to the butter mixture, alternating with the milk mixture in two additions, at medium speed. Don't overmix.

8. Scrape down the sides of the bowl and stir in the orange zest, banana, pineapple, coconut, and toasted pecans. Mix on low speed until just combined.

9. Use an ice cream scoop to fill the muffin cups three-quarters. Bake for 18 minutes or until a toothpick inserted comes out clean.

10. Cool the cakes in the pans for 10 minutes, then turn them out on a wire rack before frosting.

Nuts

When a recipe calls for "1 cup chopped pecans," this means you should chop the nuts before measuring. "1 cup nuts, chopped" means to measure the nuts, then chop them.

If you use a food processor to grind nuts for a recipe, first mix the nuts with a little flour or sugar from the recipe. That way the nuts won't turn into a paste.

Because of their high fat content, nuts can easily go rancid when exposed to oxygen and heat. Rancid nuts will ruin a recipe, so be sure to sample a few before adding to a recipe. (Savvy bakers always buy nuts from a market with rapid turnover.)

Whole, chopped, sliced, toasted or untoasted, nuts add texture and richness to cupcake recipes and decorations.

Almonds and cashews stay fresh longer than pecans and walnuts (or peanuts). Nuts in their protective shells stay fresh longer than shelled ones; whole nuts stay fresh longer than chopped nuts. Nuts will be fine in the refrigerator for about four months and about eight months in the freezer. Keep them in a sealed container so they don't absorb odors from other items. (Refrigerate your opened jar of peanut butter, too.)

TOAST NUTS FOR MAXIMUM FLAVOR

Old-fashioned way: Place nuts on a baking sheet in a 350°F oven and bake for about 5 minutes or so, until they're lightly browned. When you can smell that wonderful nutty aroma, they're done.

Modern way: Toast them in the microwave. Spread nuts in a flat dish. For ½ cup, microwave on full power for 3 or 4 minutes; a full cup for 4 to 5 minutes. Stir at least three times while cooking. The nuts will continue to darken a bit after you remove them from the microwave so don't overcook them.

Design and Recipes by Avi Sommerville

Chocolate Chip Cupcakes

Let's confess: we all know there are times when nothing will do except a glass of milk and a couple of chocolate chip cookies—unless it's one big craving-satisfying chocolate chip *cupcake*.

Materials

Chocolate Chip Cupcakes (far right)

Chocolate Sour Cream Frosting (at right)

Classic Buttercream Frosting (recipe page 20) (optional)

Semisweet chocolate chips

Chopped nuts, any kind you like

Instructions

1. Spread the cupcakes lavishly with the frosting. You can cover them all with the dark Chocolate Sour Cream Frosting or, for a contrasting look, frost some with the white Classic Buttercream Frosting.

2. With wild abandon, drop chocolate chips and nut chunks into the frosting.

3. Eat at least one before you set out the others for your guests.

Chocolate Sour Cream Frosting

1 cup milk chocolate chips
⅓ cup semisweet chocolate chips
Pinch of salt
⅔ cup sour cream

1. Place the chips and salt in a glass bowl or the top of a double boiler set over simmering (not boiling) water. Melt.

2. Mix briefly until smooth.

3. Add the sour cream all at once, and whisk it in. The mixture will seize then smooth out.

4. Remove the frosting from the heat and allow it to cool. It will thicken as it cools.

Chocolate Chip Cupcakes

8 oz (2 sticks) unsalted butter, room temperature
¾ cup sugar
¾ cup brown sugar
2 eggs
1 teaspoon vanilla extract
2 ⅓ cups flour
1 teaspoon baking soda
1 teaspoon salt
12 oz semisweet chocolate chips
1 ¼ cups milk

1. Preheat the oven to 375°F and prepare the muffin pans with nonstick spray or paper cups.

2. In the bowl of an electric mixer, combine the butter, sugars, and eggs and mix on high speed for 10 minutes. Add the vanilla.

3. Sift together the flour, baking soda, and salt and stir them into the butter mixture.

4. Stir in the chocolate chips.

5. Add the milk and stir just until combined.

6. Pour the batter into the pans, filling at least halfway. Bake for 20 to 25 minutes, or until a toothpick inserted comes out clean.

7. Turn out the cupcakes onto a wire rack to cool.

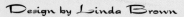

Spring Pastels

Easter-egg hues inspire a cupcake celebration of spring. Mix and match the soft frosting colors with pastel baking cups and make bunny grass from dyed coconut.

Materials

24 Classic White Cupcakes (recipe page 18)

Classic Buttercream Frosting (recipe page 20)

Food coloring

Shredded sweetened coconut, as needed

Special Tools

Pastry bag fitted with a large "open star" tip

Instructions

1. Use food coloring to make the frosting the color you want. Just add a few drops, then stir until the color is achieved. Start with only a drop or two for a pastel shade. You can always add more.

2. Put the frosting in the pastry bag. Hold the bag directly over and perpendicular to the top of a cupcake. Pipe the frosting beginning on the outside edge, then follow around the circumference and work inward, keeping the tip just above the cupcake.

3. Color the coconut by putting it in a bowl and adding one drop of the desired food coloring. Toss with latex-gloved hands, or two forks, until all the coconut is colored. Add more food coloring a little at a time until you reach the desired color. If the color is darker than desired, add more white coconut and toss as above.

4. Sprinkle coconut around the serving plate to create "grass." If you wish, sprinkle coconut on top of the frosted cupcake, pressing very lightly with your fingers to adhere it.

Design Tip

Remember that the slight ivory color of the buttercream will affect the finished color of your frostings, giving all of them a light yellow tint as the base color. For most designs this is perfectly wonderful. But if you want to have truer pastel colors for some projects, make the frosting with a brand of butter that is "whiter" than usual. A natural food store is a good source for this butter.

Design and Recipes by Charles de Vries

Apple Delight Cupcakes

Praise the magnificent apple by showing it off in three wonderful ways in one dessert. This deliciously moist cake makes a gracious end note to an elegant dinner or an unhurried brunch.

Materials

12 to 16 Applesauce Cupcakes (recipe page 40)

Orange Syrup (recipe page 40)

Coconut & Raisin Filling (recipe page 41)

12 to 16 Apple Crisps (recipe page 41)

Caramelized Apples (recipe page 40)

Confectioners' sugar

Special Tools

Pastry brush

Small sieve or strainer

Design Tip

Use the center cuts of the apple for the thin slices. The seeds leave a beautiful star design in the center of the slice.

Time-Saving Tip

The decorative Apple Crisps can be done ahead of time and stored in an airtight container.

Instructions

1. With a serrated knife, cut off the top of an Applesauce Cupcake, invert it, and cut it into slanted layers. (See the photo below.)

2. With the pastry brush, coat each layer with the Orange Syrup.

3. Spread Coconut & Raisin Filling between the layers. Chill about 30 minutes, until the filling is set.

4. Cut a slot into the top of the cupcake about 1 inch long and ¼ inch deep. Use the sieve or strainer to dust the cupcake with confectioners' sugar, then place an Apple Crisp into the slot.

5. Arrange three or more Caramelized Apple slices in a fan shape on a serving plate, or evenly space them around the cupcake.

Applesauce Cupcakes

1 ¾ cups cake flour
1 teaspoon baking soda
1 teaspoon cinnamon
½ teaspoon ground cloves
½ teaspoon salt
1 cup brown sugar
4 oz (1 stick) unsalted butter, room temperature
1 egg
1 cup applesauce
1 cup cherries, diced small
1 cup raisins

1. Preheat the oven to 350°F and prepare a muffin pan with nonstick spray. Since you want the cake to have smooth sides, don't use paper cups.

2. Sift together 1½ cups of the flour and the baking soda, cinnamon, cloves, and salt.

3. In a large bowl, cream the sugar with the butter until light.

4. Add the egg to the butter mixture and mix until blended.

5. Add the sifted dry ingredients and mix until blended.

6. Add the applesauce and mix until blended.

7. Sprinkle the remaining flour over the cherries and raisins to coat, then add to the batter.

8. Pour the batter into the muffin pan, filling each cup at least halfway. Bake 10 to 15 minutes, or until a toothpick inserted comes out clean.

9. Remove the pan and turn out the cupcakes onto a wire rack to cool.

Orange Syrup

1 cup sugar
1 cup water
1 to 2 tablespoons orange extract

1. In a saucepan, slowly dissolve the sugar in the water over medium heat, then bring to a boil.

2. Remove the syrup from the heat and add the extract. Extracts may vary considerably in strength, so begin with the small amount. When the mixture is cool enough, taste and add more extract if needed.

Caramelized Apples

2 Granny Smith apples
8 oz (2 sticks) unsalted butter, room temperature
1 cup sugar

Special Tools

Silicone mat or waxed paper

1. Cut the apples into wedges about ½ inch wide.

2. Heat the butter and sugar in a sauté pan or skillet until the butter is melted and the sugar has dissolved.

3. Add the apple wedges, and cook until the sugar browns and the apples are cooked but still hold their shape. Don't overcook.

4. Remove the apples from the caramel and cool on the silicone mat or waxed paper.

Coconut and Raisin Filling

1 cup sugar
1 tablespoon all-purpose flour
¼ teaspoon salt
12 oz evaporated milk
4 oz (1 stick) unsalted butter, room temperature
3 egg yolks, slightly beaten
1 cup flaked coconut, fresh or dried, unsweetened
½ cup pecans, chopped
1 teaspoon vanilla extract

1. In a saucepan, combine the sugar, flour, and salt, then stir in the evaporated milk.

2. Add the butter and cook over low heat, stirring, until the butter is melted.

3. Pour a small amount of the hot mixture over the slightly beaten egg yolks and mix to temper the eggs, then incorporate the tempered eggs into the mixture.

4. Stir in the coconut and pecans.

5. Cook over medium heat until thick, stirring constantly.

6. Remove the pan from the heat and add the vanilla. Set aside.

Apple Crisps

1 or 2 Granny Smith apples
1 cup water
1 cup sugar
Confectioners' sugar for dusting

Special Tools

**Kitchen mandoline
(found in specialty cooking stores)
or very sharp knife**

2 silicone mats

Baking pan

1. Preheat the oven to 250°F. Using the mandoline or a very sharp knife, cut the apple into very thin slices horizontally, making sure you have one slice for each cupcake. (Cutting across the width of the apple instead of vertically captures the design in the center left by the seeds, which will pop out as you cut.)

2. In a saucepan, bring the water and sugar to a boil. Carefully place the apple slices into the simple syrup. Let stand for 1 minute.

3. Remove the slices from the syrup and place them onto a silicone mat set on a baking pan. Cover them with another silicone mat.

4. Place the apples in the oven to dry for 30 to 40 minutes. They'll come out a lovely translucent brown.

5. Let them cool, then store the apple slices in an airtight container until ready to use.

Design by Chris Kobler. Napkin Folding Design by Terry Taylor.

Napkin-Wrapped Cupcakes

A cupcake nesting in a napkin has to look pretty as it's peeking out, and stay unfazed while the napkin is unfolded around it. The solution is a simple cupcake scooped out on the top to hold a shiny fruit glaze.

Materials

24 Easy Yellow Cupcakes (recipe page 19), unbaked

1 jar apricot preserves

1 sheet of ready-made pie dough

Edible white cake glitter

Cloth napkins, lightly starched

Special Tools

Fine mesh strainer

Small cookie cutters (optional)

Instructions

1. Fill the baking cups a little less than two-thirds full, so that the cupcakes don't rise above the rim during baking. The cakes will form a hollow in the center that will hold the glaze neatly.

2. If the cupcakes do rise above the rim, carefully slice off the tops of the cool cakes and scoop out a slight hollow with the edge of a spoon.

3. Make the apricot glaze. Push the preserves through a fine mesh strainer into a small pan and heat over low until the jam melts. If you wish, add warm water (a teaspoon at a time) to loosen the consistency, and stir thoroughly.

4. When the jam is "paintable," fill the tops of the cool cakes with an even layer of glaze.

5. Refrigerate the cakes and the apricot glaze until ready to use. When refrigerated, the glaze will return to its thicker consistency, making it easier to handle when placing it into the napkin.

6. In the meantime, bake the pie dough (follow the manufacturer's instructions) and let it chill completely. Using small cookie cutters or a sharp paring knife, cut out decorative shapes. Spread a thin coat of the apricot preserves on the tops of the shapes, then sprinkle lightly with the edible cake glitter, which will dissolve into the glaze, giving it a sheen. Place the pastry shapes on the glaze.

7. Fold and display the napkins, then carefully set the chilled cupcakes inside.

Make the Napkin Nest

1. Choose a napkin that will look pretty not only with your table setting but also with the cupcake that will be hiding inside.

Fold the napkin in half with the open edges at the bottom. Fold it in half width-wise, then crease it to make a center "line." Open it.

Bring the upper right corner down to the center line. Bring the lower left corner up to the center line.

2. Turn the napkin over and position with the folded edges at the top and bottom as shown.

3. Lift the bottom crease up to the top crease.

4. Flip out the point underneath as shown. Turn the napkin over.

5. Lift up the right flap. Bring the left flap over and crease. Fold the right flap back into position. Turn the napkin over.

6. Tuck the right point into the pocket.

7. Open up the folded napkin by placing your fingers inside the two folded edges.

1

5

2

3

6

4

7

Voila!

BAKING TIP:
Fruit

We used fruit in some way in almost a third of the recipes in the book. Not only do we love fruit, but also as busy home bakers, we rely on fruits as quick and reliable decorations.

What could be easier than topping a cupcake with a glorious crown of fresh fruit? All kinds of berries, whole or sliced, look terrific. And so do slices of peaches, pears, tangerines, pineapple, and mango. Garnish cupcake displays with any kind of fresh fruit, including berries and kiwi fruit.

Dried fruit like cherries and apricots make eye-catching garnishes for simple toppings.

Raisins are happier inside the cupcakes, especially in recipes where they get soaked with tantalizing tastes like rum or other extracts.

Zest is the sweet-flavored outer rind of citrus fruits. Tools such as microplaners help grate off the zest, without getting the bitter white part underneath. It's best to grate citrus fruits

Their variety in color, taste, and shape make fruits a favorite ingredient in cupcakes.

just before using them because the zest can dry up if it sits too long. And cold lemons are easier to grate.

FRUIT SPREADABLES

When you start decorating cupcakes, you'll soon discover the wonderful world of tasty treasures in the jelly and jam section of your grocery store.

Preserves (similar to jam) is a thick mixture of fruit and sugar, with large chunks of fruit, used as the base of fillings and glazes.

Fruit curd is a creamy mixture to which citrus fruit has been added. Lemon curd is a favorite in England and you can often find it near the jelly section. To make your own lime curd, see the directions for lime curd on page 25.

A puree is fruit that has been finely mashed to a smooth, thick consistency. It's used as the base of thin, shiny glazes.

(See also Fruit Glazes on page 51.)

Rum Raisin Bundt Cakes

Fat, juicy, rum-soaked raisins are the surprise inside these tiny bundt cakes. With convenient new bundt pans, you can make three different cake shapes at the same time. Amazing!

Materials

6 Rum Raisin Cupcakes (at right)

Thin Royal Icing (below)

Instructions

Use a ladle to pour the Thin Royal Icing over each cake. Using the photo to guide you, feel free to vary the shape of the glaze.

Thin Royal Icing

1 egg white

1 pinch cream of tartar

7 tablespoons confectioners' sugar

Lemon juice (optional)

1. Whip the egg white and cream of tartar until it's frothy. Sift in the sugar and continue whipping. The mixture will puff up quite a bit.

2. The consistency may vary. Add some lemon juice to thin it. To thicken it, add more confectioners' sugar.

Yields about 4 oz.

Rum Raisin Cupcakes

½ cup dark rum

2 tablespoons water

¼ cup raisins

7 oz plus 3 tablespoons brown sugar

4 oz (1 stick) unsalted butter, room temperature

7½ oz flour

1 ½ teaspoons baking powder

½ teaspoon salt

¼ teaspoon ground cinnamon

¼ teaspoon ground cloves

¼ teaspoon ground nutmeg

½ cup milk

2 eggs

2 teaspoons vanilla extract

Special Tools

Muffin pans with cups in the shapes of small bundt cakes (see page 11)

1. Preheat the oven to 325°F and prepare six bundt muffin cups with nonstick spray.

2. In a saucepan over medium-low heat, simmer the rum, water, raisins, and 3 tablespoons of the brown sugar, stirring occasionally. Heat until the raisins have absorbed most of the liquid. Be careful not to let the raisins burn. When they are ready, remove them from the heat and set aside. The raisins will continue to absorb liquid as they cool.

3. In the bowl of an electric mixer fitted with a paddle attachment, combine the butter with the dry ingredients until well blended.

4. Add the milk, eggs, and vanilla and mix until completely blended.

5. Gently fold in the raisins.

6. Pour the batter into the bundt cups, approximately two-thirds full. Bake for 18 to 25 minutes, or until a toothpick inserted comes out clean.

Yields 18 cupcakes

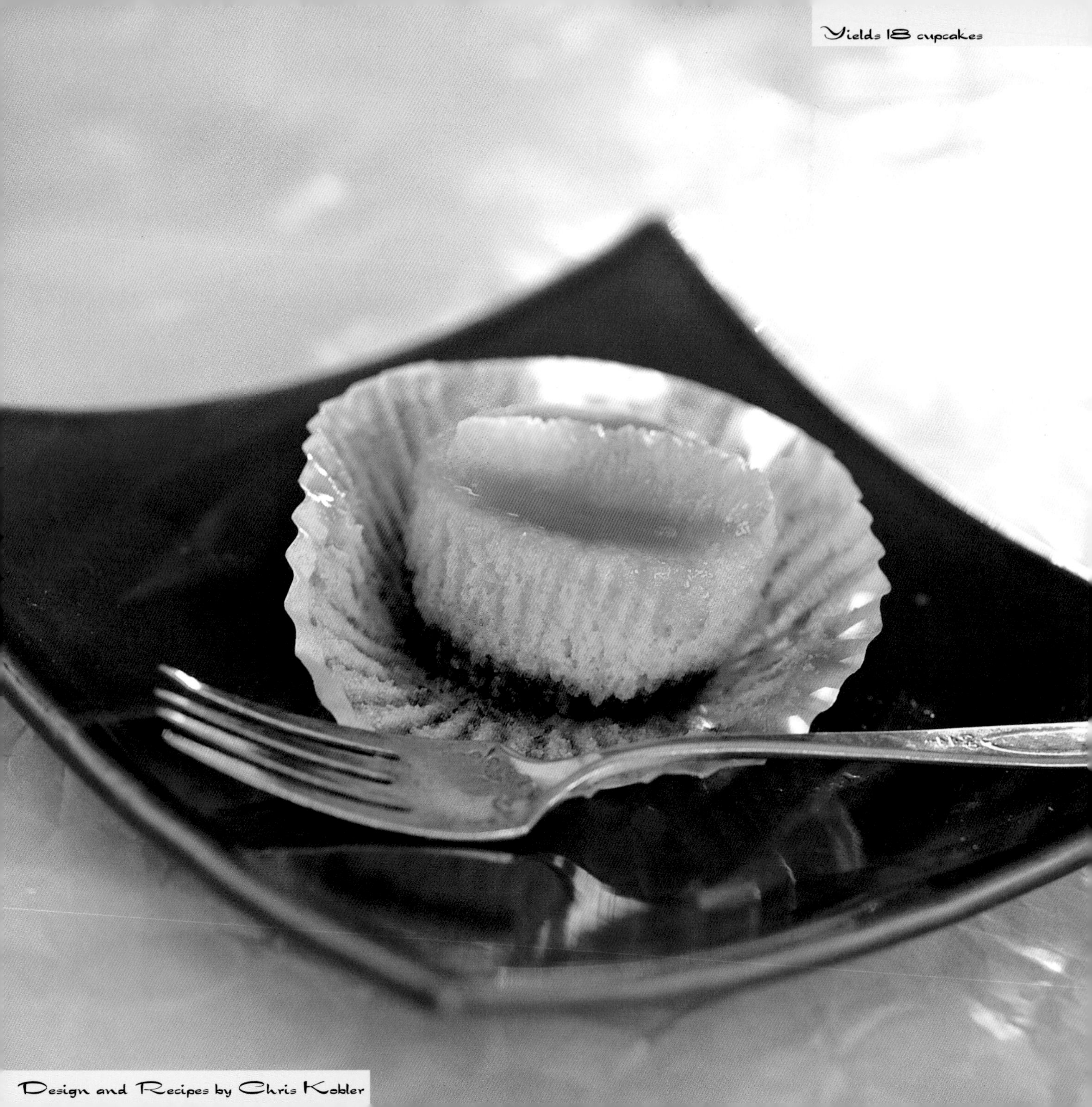

Design and Recipes by Chris Kobler

Ricotta Cheese Cupcakes

This delicately cheesy cake is full of surprises,
from its nutty bottom to its citrusy top.

Materials

**18 Ricotta Cheese Cupcakes
(recipe page 50)**

Tangerine Glaze (at right)

1 or 2 tangerines or oranges

Instructions

1. Peel, pit, and remove the
membrane of the tangerine
sections. (You can use
oranges instead of tangerines
if you wish.)

2. When the cheesecakes are
completely cool, pour enough
glaze on each cake to fill the
hollow in the top. (If the glaze
has cooled, just reheat it
until it reaches pourable
consistency.)

3. Soak the fruit sections in
the remaining glaze and place
them on top of the cakes.

4. Refrigerate the cakes at
least 1 hour to set.

Tangerine Glaze

2 tablespoons cornstarch
1 cup fresh tangerine juice
½ cup sugar
Yellow and red food coloring (optional)

1. Dissolve the cornstarch in ⅓ cup of
the juice.

2. Combine the sugar, dissolved cornstarch,
and remaining juice. If you want more color
in the glaze, add 4 drops of yellow food coloring and 1 drop of red.

3. Boil for 1 minute, then set the glaze aside
and keep it warm.

Ricotta Cheese Cupcakes

1 cup walnuts

3 tablespoons brown sugar

3 oz cream cheese

15 oz whole milk ricotta cheese

¼ cup plain yogurt

¾ cup sugar

3 eggs, separated

2 teaspoons fresh tangerine juice

1 teaspoon tangerine zest

4 tablespoons sifted cake flour

Pinch of salt

Special Tools

Food processor

1. Preheat the oven to 325°F. Prepare muffin pans with paper or foil baking cups.

2. Use a food processor to crush and combine the walnuts and brown sugar until uniform. Press 2 teaspoons of the mixture into the bottom of each baking cup.

3. In a large bowl, beat the cream cheese thoroughly, scraping the bowl several times, until completely smooth.

4. Add the ricotta cheese and yogurt and beat, scraping the bowl several times again, until completely smooth.

5. Beat in the sugar, then beat in the egg yolks, juice, and zest.

6. Gradually mix in the flour and salt.

7. In a separate bowl, beat the egg whites until stiff, but not dry, and fold in thoroughly.

8. Pour the mixture into the baking cups, filling each one three-quarters.

9. Bake until set and just barely colored, 30 to 35 minutes.

10. Turn off the oven and leave the cakes inside for an hour to cool slowly. The centers may curve downward a bit. That's okay, because you're going to fill the cavity with a delicious topping.

A coating of fruit syrup keeps fillings tasty and distinct.

A fruit glaze, which pastry chefs refer to as *nappage*, makes a terrific quick cupcake topping and is useful in other ways, too. The simplest form is melted jam or jelly that you've first thinned through a strainer. Sieved apricot jam is traditionally used for white and yellow fruits and red currant jelly for red fruits.

Warm citrus glazes add a glow to spicy cakes.

Melted apricot jam is the "glue" holding fondant to the cake.

Glazes heighten the color of fresh fruit and make them shine.

Design and Recipe by Chris Kobler

Winter Spice Cupcakes with Snowflakes

Welcome your holiday visitors with yummy old-fashioned spice cakes covered with powdered sugar snowflakes. They're so much fun to decorate, why not have your guests help you?

Materials

Winter Spice Cupcakes, cooled (recipe page 54)

Sheet of sturdy paper or clear acetate and pencil for making stencils

Confectioners' sugar

Special Tools

Craft knife

Cutting mat (optional)

Small sieve

Instructions

1. It's easy to make stencils. Find an image with enough open space to create a pleasing design with the confectioners' sugar. Draw it on a sheet of paper or, to make it more permanent, on a piece of clear acetate. Be sure to add a "handle" so your stencil will be easier to lift. Make stencils to fit each size cupcake you want to cover.

2. Use the craft knife and a safe cutting surface (such as the cutting mat in the photo below) to cut out the shapes.

3. Fill a small sieve with confectioners' sugar. Center a stencil on the top of a completely cooled cupcake. Holding the sieve with one hand, position it over the cake and tap it gently with the forefinger of your other hand until an even, solid layer of sugar covers the cake. (Make it thick enough to cover the cake nicely, but not so thick that it will blow off and ruin your design as soon as you move the cupcake. Practice makes perfect.)

4. To keep the sugar design intact, smoothly lift the stencil straight up off the cake (having a handle on the stencil helps), keeping it steady so sugar doesn't fall off.

5. Being careful that your fingertips don't mar the stenciled sugar, arrange the cupcakes on a display plate.

Design Tip

You can make designs with both the positive and negative space of the cutout. It looks elegant to mix the styles, as you can see in the photos.

Time-Saving Tip

Keep a supply of stencils on hand for last-minute decorating, such as hearts, stars, and letters of the alphabet to spell Happy Birthday.

Winter Spice Cupcakes

2 ½ cups all-purpose flour
2 teaspoons baking soda
2 teaspoons freshly ground cardamom
1 teaspoon freshly ground cinnamon
1 teaspoon freshly ground coriander seed
Pinch of salt
1 tablespoon fine lemon zest
4 oz (1 stick) unsalted butter, room temperature
½ cup brown sugar
2 large eggs
1 cup pomegranate molasses, available at gourmet or Middle Eastern food stores (or substitute unsulphured molasses)
1 cup boiling water

Note: The recipe yields 18 cupcakes, or 36 mini-cupcakes, or 10 jumbo cupcakes. Make several batches and mix sizes.

1. Preheat the oven to 350°F and prepare a muffin pan with nonstick spray or paper cups.

2. Sift together the flour, baking soda, spices, salt, and lemon zest. (To make the zest fine enough to pass through the sieve, mince the pieces after scraping the zest from the rind.)

3. In a large bowl, cream the butter until fluffy. Add the sugar, and beat until fluffy again. Scrape down the sides with a rubber spatula several times during this process.

4. Add the eggs and molasses, and beat well. Carefully stir in the boiling water until the mixture is smooth. When combined, gradually add the dry ingredients, stirring to incorporate after each addition.

5. Fill the muffin cups three-quarters. Bake for 20 to 25 minutes, or until a toothpick inserted comes out clean.

6. If you're baking mini cupcakes, they'll take less time, of course, so begin to test them after 15 minutes.

The most common spices for baking are often used in combination with one another. Use the form of spice—whole, grated, or ground—called for in the recipe.

Cardamom, the ground seed of a tree in the ginger family, has a pungent, gingery taste.

Cinnamon, the most common baking spice, is the dried bark of a tree native to Sri Lanka. It has a warm, spicy flavor popular in cold weather recipes.

Cloves are the dried unopened buds of an evergreen tree native to the Malucca Islands in Indonesia. They have a pungent, sweet aroma.

Coriander seeds, from the parsley family, have a distinctive sweet lemony flavor.

Ginger, from the underground stem of a tropical plant, has a sweet spicy flavor.

55

Though tiny in amount, spices give cupcakes an enormous tastebud boost. They're best when freshly grated or ground.

Nutmeg is an aromatic seed produced by an evergreen tree native to the same Indonesian Islands as the source of cloves.

Poppy seeds, from the poppy flower, have a sweet nutlike flavor that goes well with light cake.

Salt in the forms of common table salt, kosher salt, and sea salt can be used interchangeably in recipes. If stored in an airtight container, it will keep indefinitely.

Vanilla bean is the pod of a climbing orchid native to Mexico. Its extract is a standard ingredient in cupcake recipes, both cake and frosting.

Measure spices by placing them in a measuring spoon and leveling off with a knife or spatula. A dash of a spice means about $1/16$ teaspoon.

Store spices in airtight containers in a cool, dark place, away from moisture, heat and direct sunlight. Whole spices stay fresh for about two years, ground spices for about a year.

To check for freshness-open the container of spice—if it has a strong pungent fragrance, it's fresh.

Design and Recipe by Chris Kobler

Dramatic
Two-Tone Cupcakes

What could be more suitable for an opening night celebration than these black and white cupcakes with a dazzling strawberry topping? Don't be surprised if it's you who gets most of the evening's applause!

Materials

12 Easy Yellow Cupcakes (recipe page 19)

White and Chocolate Dipping Fondant (recipes page 58), kept warm and pourable

1 jar currant jelly

1 pint fresh strawberries

Special Tools

Wire cooling rack placed over waxed paper

Pastry brush

Note: After you make the dipping fondant (page 58), it will stay warm and pourable for about 20 minutes. If it hardens, just beat it by hand. If necessary, add 1 or 2 teaspoons of hot water and continue beating until it returns to pourable consistency.

Instructions

1. With a dinner fork, spear a cupcake through its top, holding it in one hand. With the other hand, tilt the bowl of white fondant so it pools and immerse one side of the cupcake into it. (See the photo below.) Carefully lift out the cupcake and let as much fondant as possible drain back into the bowl. Put the cake right side up on the cooling rack and carefully remove the fork.

2. When the white fondant has dried a bit, about 2 minutes, just as it loses its glossiness, repeat the process in step 1 to cover the other side with the chocolate fondant.

3. Don't worry about trying to cover the top (which will be covered with strawberries) or the bottom. Coat the sides with a straight, clean line where the chocolate meets the white, or let a hint of the cake peek through.

4. When all the cakes have been coated and the fondant dried, melt the currant jelly and lightly spread it on the cake tops. The jelly will help hold the strawberries in place and inhibit the "bleeding" of fruit juice into the fondant icing.

5. Slice the strawberries or leave them whole, as you wish. Place them on top of the cakes and use the pastry brush to paint the berries lightly with the melted jelly to glaze and brighten them.

White and Chocolate Dipping Fondant

(enough for 12 cakes)

½ cup hot water

¼ cup light corn syrup

5 cups confectioners' sugar

½ teaspoon vanilla extract

2 oz unsweetened chocolate, chopped

Special Tools

**2 deep rimless bowls or
small mixing bowls**

2 sauce pans

1. In a saucepan, combine the water and corn syrup and bring to a boil.

2. Remove the mixture from the heat and stir in the sugar until it's completely smooth. Stir in the vanilla.

3. Stir in small amounts of additional hot water until the consistency of the fondant is like warm honey.

4. Pour half the fondant, which is now bright white, into one of the mixing bowls.

5. Put the chocolate pieces in the other bowl and hold it over hot water in the other sauce pan while you pour the remaining fondant over it. Stir until the chocolate is melted and smooth and the entire mixture has the same honeylike consistency as the white fondant.

Baking with Chocolate

Alas, life isn't fair: The best baking chocolate doesn't come cheap. Imported chocolate and the best of the domestic brands can be costly, but there's really no comparison between the best baking chocolate and the lower-cost alternatives. If you're a chocolate lover on a budget, our advice is to always enjoy the best chocolate, just do so on fewer occasions.

The best quality baking chocolate comes in big chunks—dark, semisweet, milk, and white. Cocoa powder is unsweetened. Dark ground chocolate comes both sweetened and unsweetened.

TEMPERING CHOCOLATE

Certain recipes call for tempered chocolate, which means you need to stabilize the chocolate through a melt-and-cool process called *tempering*. This process makes the chocolate more malleable and glossy. Store-bought chocolate is already tempered, but this changes when you melt it, because the fat in the chocolate's cocoa butter forms crystals that can produce dull gray streaks called *bloom*.

Here's our best advice on how to temper chocolate easily. First, you need good quality chocolate. If you're using a bar chocolate, be sure to read the ingredients. If the chocolate contains any additives, fillers, or fats besides cocoa butter, don't use it. It won't temper. A good workable amount of chocolate to temper is about 1½ pounds.

1. Chop the chocolate into small chunks, about the size of a bean, which is a size that will melt easily. Use a chocolate chopper with metal tines, or a thick, sharp knife.

2. Place the chocolate in a clean, dry bowl (any moisture in the bowl will ruin the process) and place that bowl over (not in) a pot of simmering (not boiling) water. Don't cover the chocolate; any steam that collects could also ruin the process, causing the chocolate to seize or curdle.

3. Use a candy thermometer to check the temperature. Dark chocolate should be heated to 120°F, milk or white chocolate to 110°F. Melt two-thirds of the chocolate to the appropriate temperature, then add the remaining one-third, stirring until the mixture drops to 89°F and is smooth and glossy.

Chocolate Ganache Cupcakes

Chocolate cake, chocolate ganache, chocolate spikes–chocolate, chocolate!

Materials

12 Chocolate Buttermilk Cupcakes (recipe page 19)

Dark Chocolate Ganache (recipe at right)

Milk Chocolate Ganache (recipe at right)

Chocolate Spikes (recipe at right)

Special Tools

Muffin pan with square cups (optional)

Pizza wheel (optional)

Double boiler

Instructions

1. If you want the distinctly different square shape, you have two options. Use a silicone muffin pan with square cups, or do the old-fashioned thing and, when the cakes are cool, use a sharp knife to slice the tops and sides square.

2. Place the cooled cupcakes on a wire rack with a baking sheet underneath.

3. Use a ladle to pour the Dark Chocolate Ganache over the cupcakes to cover all the edges. Let it set about 10 minutes on each cake.

4. Using a fork, drizzle the Milk Chocolate Ganache over each cupcake in one direction. Turn the cupcake the opposite direction and drizzle again. Refrigerate the cakes until serving time.

5. When it's time to serve the cakes, place the spikes on top as desired.

6. In warm weather, the spikes will start melting pretty quickly, making some wild unplanned shapes—enjoy!

Dark Chocolate Ganache

4 oz good quality bittersweet dark chocolate

4 oz heavy cream

1. Chop the chocolate fine and place it in a small bowl.

2. Bring the cream in a small pot to a simmer.

3. Pour the simmering cream over the chopped chocolate and stir until smooth.

4. Cool to room temperature

Milk Chocolate Ganache

4 oz good quality milk chocolate

4 oz heavy cream

Follow the same directions as the Dark Chocolate Ganache above.

Chocolate Spikes

2 oz good quality dark chocolate

1. Melt the chocolate in the top of a double boiler.

2. Line a baking sheet with parchment paper and pour the melted chocolate on it. Spread the chocolate evenly, then let it set.

3. Use the pizza wheel or a sharp knife to cut slices of chocolate.

4. Refrigerate until just before serving.

Design and Recipes by Sarah and Peter Hall

Butterfly Cupcakes

What an unforgettable garden party it will be when stunning butterflies come to perch atop your chocolate cupcakes. Made of melted sugar and frosting, the little beauties are completely edible, so they're perfect decorations when your guests include both adults and children.

Materials

12 Chocolate Buttermilk Cupcakes (recipe page 19)

Sugar Mixture (recipe at right)

Royal Icing (recipe page 65), dyed black

Parchment paper to make disposable pastry bags

Egg carton

Aluminum foil

Protective gloves

Towel

Confectioners' sugar

Special Tools

Star tip for pastry bag

Small sieve

Note: Budget enough time to make this project. The butterfly bodies need overnight to harden.

Make Pastry Bags

See instructions on page 101 on how to make parchment paper pastry bags. Make a bag for each color of sugar you want to pipe on the butterfly wings.

Make the Egg Carton Holder

1. Invert an empty egg carton and line the ridges with aluminum foil.

2. Inside each foil ridge, place a bit of parchment paper (see photos 64).

Make the Sugar Mixture

2 cups sugar
⅓ cup water
Food coloring

Special Tools

Candy thermometer

1. In a small saucepan, mix the sugar and water to achieve wet sand consistency.

2. Heat until the sugar is completely dissolved. Add a few drops of food coloring in your choice of color.

3. Using the candy thermometer, boil the sugar mixture to 240°F (yes, that's the exact temperature) and remove it from the heat.

4. Allow the mixture to cool slightly until a honeylike consistency is achieved.

5. This recipe will make about 15 pairs of medium-size wings.

63

Make the Sugar Wings

1. You'll need to wear protective gloves, such as latex dishwashing gloves, to protect your hands from the hot sugar inside the pastry bag. Also, have a thick towel handy.

2. Place your piping bag tip down into a sturdy glass or coffee mug. As soon as the sugar mixture has reached the honeylike consistency, pour it into the piping bag. If the sugar is too thick to pour, simply heat it back up until it is pourable.

3. Roll down the top of the piping bag to secure the sugar in it and cut a tiny hole off the tip of the bag.

4. Wrap the towel around the bag and pipe your wings onto a flat sheet of parchment paper. First pipe the outline of the wings, then pipe back and forth to make the insides. You'll have to move as quickly as possible because the sugar will start to harden in just a few moments. Make as many wings as you can before you have to refill the bag with hot melted sugar. Change pastry bags as often as you want to change color.

5. Set the wings aside on the parchment paper to harden.

6. For the larger wings, first pipe an outline in one color and then fill it in with different colored sugars prepared in the same fashion. Have fun creating different sizes and shapes. Use the photos to guide you.

Make the Butterfly Bodies

1. Fill a parchment pastry bag with Royal Icing (recipe on opposite page) that you've dyed black with food color. Using a star tip, pipe the bodies onto the parchment paper on the egg carton holder.

2. Gently slide two matching hardened-sugar butterfly wings into the sides of one of the bodies, allowing the wings to rest against the sides of the foil ridges. Repeat for all the butterfly wings and bodies.

3. Allow the bodies to harden overnight.

Assemble the Display

1. Using the sieve, sift a bit of confectioners' sugar over the tops of each cooled cupcake. (See the sugar sifting directions on page 53.)

2. With a serrated knife cut a deep, narrow slice into the top of the cupcake.

3. Very carefully, remove the butterflies from the egg carton holder.

4. Pipe a dab of the black Royal Icing in the slot as a fixative, and gently press the butterfly to the top of the cake.

5. Allow time for drying, then move the cupcakes to a display plate and serve.

Royal Icing

This is the basic, all-purpose icing you find on most bakery cakes. It also serves as the glue that holds decorations to the cupcakes in some projects, and it works well for piping and rosettes. This recipe is for approximately 1 cup and can be increased as specified in project instructions.

You may want to vary the consistency according to use. To make the icing stiffer (for piping or decorations), gradually add more sugar. To make it softer (for spreading), add water by sprinkling just a few drops at a time, then beating until it is the desired consistency.

You may color the icing with liquid food coloring. If you plan to use it as white icing, add a drop of blue food coloring to the mixture to counteract the icing's natural grayish tint.

It is extremely important to use a perfectly clean bowl and beaters and/or spoons when making Royal Icing. Even a small bit of grit will cause the egg whites to collapse. Rinse your utensils with boiling water, then thoroughly dry. Using a copper bowl will help to stabilize the egg whites.

1 ¾ cups confectioners' sugar

1 egg white

1 teaspoon lemon juice

1. Sift the sugar.

2. In a clean bowl, beat the egg white until stiff, but not dry. If you are using an electric beater (recommended when you increase the quantity), keep the machine at its lowest speed and be careful not to overbeat.

3. Gradually add the sifted sugar and lemon juice to the egg white, beating well to blend after each addition. The final consistency should be thick but soft, like whipped cream.

4. Cover the icing with a damp cloth and set it aside until ready to use. It can be stored in the refrigerator, covered, for two days. Always beat lightly before using after the icing has been sitting.

Design and Recipe by Jane Tomlinson

Crystallized Flowers

A thin coat of sugar turns edible flowers into exquisite candies. If kept safely stored, the crystallized flowers can be used to give cupcakes a hint of summer all the way into winter.

Materials

12 Classic White or Easy Yellow Cupcakes (recipes pages 18 or 19)

Ivory Buttercream Frosting (recipe page 21)

Crystallized edible flowers, as many as desired

Green food coloring (optional)

Special Tools

Pastry bag with #67 tip (optional)

Instructions

1. Frost the cooled cupcakes with the Ivory Buttercream Frosting.

2. Place the crystallized flowers on the frosting.

3. If you wish, add a few drops of green food coloring to any leftover frosting and use the pastry bag to pipe a few leaves around the flowers. (You may need to add a little more confectioners' sugar to the frosting to get a firmer consistency for piping.)

Time-Saving Tip

At your grocery store, you can find a can of green-tinted decorator frosting, complete with a decorating tip with a built-in nozzle, that's perfect for leaves.

Note: Because the crystallized flowers need to dry completely before you use them, plan to make them at least two days before they're needed.

Edible Flowers for Crystallization

During crystallization, flowers with fragile petals can curl or crumple. The following edible flowers and herbs crystallize well:

Carnations

Cornflowers

Daisies

Lavender

Lilac

Pansies

Roses, including separate rose petals and miniature roses

Violas

Note: See information on edible flowers in the Pansies in Buttercream project on page 136.

Crystallize the Flowers

Materials

12 large edible flowers (see list on previous page for suggested varieties), or as many small ones as desired

Superfine sugar (make your own by grinding regular sugar in a blender)

1 egg white

Special Tools

Small strainer

Soft sable artist's paintbrush

Cooling rack or screen with small grids, sprayed with a nonstick spray

Airtight container

Instructions

1. Prepare your work area with one bowl filled with sugar and the other next to it empty. Strain the egg white into a cup (to break up its natural viscosity). Hold a flower by its stem. Using the paintbrush, coat the flower completely, front and back, with the egg white.

2. Hold the flower over the empty bowl and spoon sugar over it, coating it completely. Tap the flower lightly on the sides of the bowl several times to remove excess or any clumps of sugar.

3. Place the flower on the rack or screen to dry. Repeat for all flowers, and allow them to dry for 24 to 48 hours (depending on the humidity). Store sugared flowers in an airtight container if not using immediately.

BAKING TIP:

Sweeteners

The use of sweeteners is the primary diference between cake and bread. Most cake recipes call for plain old granulated white sugar, which is of the right consistency to enter into batter and frostings well, and it's readily available. Special recipes use other sweeteners, each of which has a different purpose and taste.

Bakers love the wide range of sweeteners used in recipes around the world, such as (clockwise) turbinado sugar, maple syrup, corn syrup, honey, confectioners' sugar (often called powdered or icing sugar), brown sugar, molasses, and granulated sugar.

Low-Sugar Sweetener

Thanks to the development of a low-sugar granulated sweetener that is also safe for diabetics, many more people can now become cupcake lovers. Sucralose is derived from sugar cane, but it's modified and thus not recognized by the body as sugar.

It has no effect on blood glucose levels, carbohydrate metabolism, or insulin secretion. You can use sucralose in a similar (not exactly the same) way you use sugar in recipes. For every cup of sucralose, add ½ cup sifted nonfat dry milk powder and ½ teaspoon baking soda and add them to the dry ingredients. Cupcakes baked with sucralose may bake a littler faster, so check for doneness a few minutes earlier. As you would with any unfamiliar ingredient, follow the manufacturer's information and experiment.

Design and Glaze Recipe by Chris Kobler

Mardi Gras Party Cakes

The Mardi Gras merrymaking begins when you bring out cupcakes decorated in the traditional "king cake" colors of green, yellow, and purple. In the New Orleans spirit of *lagniappe*—putting a little extra on the plate–make plenty of extras for guests to take home.

Materials

12 cupcakes, any flavor you like, in festive gold foil baking cups

Sugar Glaze (at right)

Sanding sugars in green, purple, and yellow

Stiff piece of paper

Design Tip

You may flavor the glaze with extracts, juices, or liqueurs, substituting juices and liqueurs one to one for the cream. Use no more than ½ teaspoon extract with this quantity or the glaze may become bitter.

Instructions

1. When they are completely cooled, carefully hold each cupcake and dip its crown into the glaze, letting the excess drip back into the bowl.

2. While the glaze is still wet (within 1 to 3 minutes), sprinkle the glaze with three different colored bands of sanding sugar and allow them to set. (See tips at right on how to make distinct bold stripes with the sanding sugars.)

3. Repeat for each cupcake.

Sugar Glaze

1 ½ cups confectioners' sugar
2 to 4 tablespoons cream
1 tablespoon unsalted butter, melted and slightly cooled but still liquid

1. In a medium mixing bowl, combine the confectioners' sugar with 2 tablespoons of the cream and beat with a whisk until smooth.

2. Add the melted butter and continue beating until smooth.

3. If needed, add more cream to achieve (and maintain) pouring consistency.

71

How to Make Sugar Stripes

1. Hold a stiff piece of paper to mask two-thirds of the cupcake as you sprinkle the first color down the paper onto the top of a cupcake that has been covered with sugar glaze to make it slightly sticky.

2. Move the mask to cover the last third as you sprinkle the middle band.

3. Turn the cake around, mask the two sections you have already colored, and sprinkle the final section.

Caterpillar & Friends

Bring on the bugs! Kids love the crawly shapes and crayon-colored frostings, and adults are keen to figure out how you made them. Choux pastry—used in eclairs and cream puffs—makes unique and tasty body parts.

Materials

Any cupcake recipe you like. See Classic White, Easy Yellow, or Chocolate Buttermilk Cupcakes (recipes pages 18 and 19).

Classic Buttercream Frosting (recipe page 20), quantity to match the number of cupcakes you make

Choux Pastry Body Parts (recipe page 74)

Special baking food coloring, your choice of colors

Dragée balls (found in specialty stores)

Special Tools

Pastry bags and small tips

Instructions

1. Dye the buttercream frosting in as many colors as you want to spread on the cupcakes, which will be the bugs' bodies.

2. Frost each cupcake, then use the pastry bags to pipe on designs and features in contrasting colors. Use your imagination, photos from books, or the project photos as guides.

3. Gently press the choux pastry body parts into the frosting, as needed.

4. Add final touches, such as dragée ball eyeballs.

Design Tip

To get the saturated color in the design, don't use the food coloring you find in grocery stores, which really won't provide enough color. Use pastes, powders, or gels made especially for intense baking colors—you'll find them in specialty baking stores or the baking section of craft stores.

Design Tip

Notice that the caterpillar actually has a smaller, fake head on its tail end—pretty clever protective camouflage, eh? Kids love these kinds of details.

Choux Pastry Body Parts

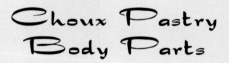

½ cup water

2 tablespoons (¼ stick) unsalted butter, room temperature

⅛ teaspoon salt

½ cup flour

2 eggs

Special Tools

Parchment paper

Electric mixer with a paddle attachment

Pastry bag with small tip

1. Preheat the oven to 350°F and line a baking sheet with parchment paper.

2. Boil the water, butter, and salt together. Add the flour, all at once. Stir the mixture with a wooden spoon. It will congeal and turn into a ball. Continue to stir around the pan until a film begins to form on the pan and it smells like baking bread (indicating that the flour is beginning to "cook").

3. Take the dough ball out of the pan and put it in the bowl of the electric mixer. Using the paddle blade, mix vigorously and add the eggs. The mixture will become silky smooth and well blended.

4. Put some batter into the pastry bag and pipe insect parts in the shapes you want (such as spider legs and big antennae) onto the parchment paper-lined baking sheet. Bake for 5 minutes or so, just until lightly browned.

Celtic Spiral Cardholders

Personalize your party cupcakes with
easy-to-make wire cardholders.

18mm gauge copper wire

Wire cutters

Small needle-nose pliers

Glass beads of 2 sizes for each holder

Pretty paper to make name cards

1. Cut the wire into 10-inch lengths for each holder.

2. Using the pliers, pinch one end of the cut wire and curl it into a spiral.

3. Keep on curling, leaving a gap of about ⅛ inch between each curl. After you've made four curves, bend the wire straight down.

4. Place the large bead, then the smaller one, onto the straightened wire just below the spiral. With the pliers, twist the wire into a small coil to support the beads.

5. Straighten the wire below the coil and cut it to the desired height.

6. Cut or tear pieces of the paper and write your guests' names on them. Insert between the spirals.

Design by Emma Pearson

Design and Icing Recipe by Sarah and Peter Hall

Flirty Flowers

Delicate, charming, and irresistible—these classic flower cupcakes are flirty favorites for all occasions. Women love their dainty prettiness. Men love the simple water icing that makes them easy to eat.

Ivory Water Icing

4 cups confectioners' sugar
Water
Ivory food coloring

1. In a small bowl, mix the confectioners' sugar with a few drops of water at a time to form a thick yet workable icing.

2. Add a tiny amount of ivory food coloring and stir until it's the shade you want.

Materials

24 chocolate cupcakes (see Chocolate Buttermilk Cupcakes on page 19), baked in paper cups

Ivory Water Icing (recipe at right)

Royal Icing (recipe page 65)

Food coloring in pastels, including green

Special Tools

1 or more pastry bags with tips in star and leaf shapes

Instructions

1. Let the cupcakes cool on a cooling rack placed over waxed paper. When they're cool, use a small ladle to pour the Ivory Water Icing over them. Allow the icing to drip artfully over the sides.

2. Pour a little Royal Icing into separate containers, and mix in food coloring to achieve pastel flower colors; also make a pale green color for the leaves.

3. Place one color of Royal Icing in a pastry bag, and using a star-shaped tip, pipe the flower on top. Do all the flowers of one color on different cupcakes at one time, then another color, and so on. Clean the pastry bag after each color or use a separate bag.

4. Fill a pastry bag with green icing, attach a leaf tip, and pipe three leaves around each flower.

5. Allow time for the icing to set before serving.

Design Tip

We chose pink, pale yellow, and ivory to create a delicate pastel look. But you can use dramatic colors such as red, orange, and purple for a more show-off display.

Consider other easy-to-make designs such as shamrocks, stars, or seashells.

Time-Saving Tip

Instead of using the same pastry bag and washing it out after each application of a different color, make simple pastry bags out of parchment paper and dispose of them when you're finished decorating. See page 101 for instructions.

Poppy Seed & Almond Cupcakes

These sassy cupcakes are special and not a bit shy about strutting their stuff. They're made with potato starch flour instead of wheat flour, which means anyone on a gluten-free diet can enjoy them.

Materials

16 Poppy Seed Gluten-Free Cupcakes (recipe at right)

Apricot Buttercream Frosting (recipe below)

1 cup sliced almonds

Time-Saving Tip

These are great make-ahead cupcakes—in fact, some people prefer the texture of the cake when it's a day old. (But if you like angel food cake, you'll like it best the same day it's baked.)

Instructions

1. Cover the cooled cupcakes generously with the Apricot Buttercream Frosting.

2. Decorate with the sliced almonds.

Apricot Buttercream Frosting

2 cups Classic Buttercream Frosting
(see page 20)

⅓ to ½ cup apricot spreadable fruit
(found in jelly section)

Mix the ingredients with a spoon until thoroughly blended and smooth.

Poppy Seed Gluten-Free Cupcakes

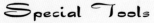

½ cup sliced almonds

½ cup potato starch flour
(available at health food stores)

6 tablespoons sugar

2 tablespoons poppy seeds

5 eggs

¾ cup confectioners' sugar

3 tablespoons unsalted butter, melted

Special Tools

Food processor or blender

Electric mixer

1. Preheat the oven to 350°F and prepare muffin pans with 16 paper baking cups.

2. Combine the almonds, potato starch, and sugar in the food processor, and grind until it reaches a fine texture similar to cornmeal.

3. Add the poppy seeds and pulse briefly, just to combine them.

4. In the bowl of an electric mixer, beat the eggs until they're frothy.

5. Add the confectioners' sugar and continue beating until light, fluffy, and pale yellow. If you lift the beater, the egg mixture should fall back in the bowl in a ribbon that remains visible on top of the batter for several seconds.

6. Gently fold the almond mixture into the eggs in three batches. The goal is to retain as much volume as possible while incorporating the ingredients thoroughly.

7. Fold the melted butter into the batter.

8. Fill the paper baking cups halfway with batter.

9. Bake for 15 to 20 minutes, or until a toothpick inserted comes out clean.

Chocolate Mousse Layered Cake

An utterly delicious chocolate mousse layered cake waits to be discovered under its lacy chocolate dome—won't your special guest be enchanted?

Materials

Chocolate Sponge Cupcakes (page 82)

Chocolate Syrup (page 82)

Chocolate Mousse (page 83)

Milk Chocolate Ganache (page 83)

8 oz semisweet or bittersweet chocolate

Vegetable oil, such as canola, with no flavor

1 oz shaved white chocolate

Chopped toasted nuts, ½ cup

Special Tools

Pastry brush

Pastry bag with a small round tip

4-inch-diameter balloon, 1 for each dome

Instructions

1. With a serrated knife, cut the rounded top off the baked and cooled cupcake.

2. Turn the cupcake over and slice it into three equal layers.

3. Brush the Chocolate Syrup over each layer, letting the syrup soak into the cake.

4. Spread the Chocolate Mousse on top of each layer.

5. Stack the iced layers (three layers per cupcake). Refrigerate or freeze until the mousse has hardened on the top layer and then cover the entire cake with plastic wrap. (Doing it this way will prevent the mousse from sticking to the plastic wrap.) Freeze the cupcakes for at least 1 hour before proceeding.

6. While the cupcakes are freezing, make the Chocolate Dome (see next page).

7. When you are ready to assemble, warm up the Milk Chocolate Ganache.

8. Place the cupcakes on a wire rack over parchment paper and pour ganache over them.

9. Chill them for at least 10 minutes in the refrigerator.

10. The ganache will be sticky enough to hold the toasted nuts, so just cup them in your hand and press them onto the bottom sides of the cupcake.

11. Place the cupcake on a pretty plate. Sprinkle shaved white chocolate on and around it and place the Chocolate Dome over it.

Note: The recipe for sponge cake will make 12 cupcakes, but it's likely you'll want to serve fewer of these dramatic domed delicacies at any one time. You can freeze the extra cupcakes (soaked in the Chocolate Syrup, if you wish) and any leftover ganache separately, then pop them out at a later date, defrost, ice the cakes with the ganache, and enjoy an instant treat. Extra mousse will not freeze so successfully, but it can be refrigerated for a day or two and served on its own or with a cookie accompaniment.

Make the Chocolate Dome

1. Temper the semisweet or bittersweet chocolate. (See notes on tempering chocolate on page 59.)

2. Place the tempered chocolate into the pastry bag with a small round tip.

3. Inflate, tie off, and lightly coat with vegetable oil one balloon for each serving.

4. Pipe the chocolate onto the balloon in a pretty lacy pattern (use the photo as a guide) or choose a design of your own, such as Art Deco angles or a flower and leaf design.

5. Place the balloon in a cool area, 65 to 75°F, for 3 to 5 minutes to dry and harden. You can set it upright in a muffin pan, making sure the chocolate doesn't touch the pan. Don't put it in the refrigerator unless the room is warmer than 80°F. (If your room is warmer than 80°F, well, you're going to have a hard time tempering chocolate anyway!)

6. When the chocolate dome has hardened, deflate the balloon by pricking it with a pair of scissors near the tied end, so the air will escape slowly. (If you prick the balloon in its wide center, it will deflate too quickly and perhaps damage the dome.)

7. Discard the balloon and set the dome to rest on a flat surface.

Time-Saving Tips

Make the chocolate dome ahead of time and store it in an airtight container in a cool dry place, such as a pantry or kitchen closet. Be sure to keep it away from direct heat and light.

Chocolate Sponge Cupcakes

1 cup unsweetened cocoa powder
5 tablespoons all-purpose flour
4 tablespoons cornstarch
6 egg whites
1 cup sugar, divided in half
10 egg yolks
9 tablespoons (2 ⅛ sticks) unsalted butter, melted

1. Preheat the oven to 350°F and prepare a muffin pan with nonstick spray and flour.

2. Sift together the cocoa, flour, and cornstarch and set aside.

3. Whip the egg whites to medium peaks, then slowly add ½ cup of the sugar and whip to soft peaks.

4. Whip the egg yolks and remaining ½ cup sugar to a thick ribbon stage.

5. Fold the egg yolks into the egg white mixture.

6. Fold the sifted dry ingredients into the egg mixture.

7. Fold in the butter.

8. Pour the batter into the muffin pan, filling the cups at least halfway. Bake for 15 to 20 minutes, or until a toothpick inserted comes out clean.

9. Remove the pan and turn out the cupcakes onto a wire rack to cool.

Chocolate Syrup

1 cup water

½ cup sugar

¼ cup cocoa

1. Mix the ingredients in a saucepan.

2. Bring the mixture to a boil while stirring.

3. Remove from the heat.

Chocolate Mousse

1 egg

2 egg yolks

⅓ cup sugar

2 tablespoons water

1 cup heavy cream

6 oz dark chocolate, melted

2 oz (½ stick) unsalted butter, softened

Milk Chocolate Ganache

1 oz (¼ stick) unsalted butter, room temperature

¼ cup heavy cream

5 oz milk chocolate

¼ teaspoon vanilla extract

1. Heat the butter and cream to scalding.

2. Put the chocolate in a heat-resistant bowl. Pour the cream and butter mixture over the chocolate and mix until smooth.

3. Add the vanilla and stir to incorporate.

1. In the bowl of an electric mixer, combine the egg and egg yolks, whipping slightly.

2. In a saucepan, heat the sugar and water to 234°F (the exact melting temperature), or "soft ball" stage.

3. Slowly pour the sugar syrup into the eggs, whipping on slow speed as you do.

When all the syrup has been added, turn to high and whip until cool.

4. In a separate bowl, whip the cream to medium peaks, then fold it into the egg mixture.

5. Combine the melted chocolate and butter, then fold it into the egg mixture.

Design and Recipe by Chris Kobler

Key Lime Cup Tarts

When bakers in early Key West, Florida discovered that the local lime—the very sour key lime–curdled milk and eggs without using heat, the classic key lime pie was born. Here's a modern cupcake version that's sure to please lime-lovers everywhere.

Materials

Key Lime Tarts (recipe at right)

Fresh lime

Instructions

1. With a sharp knife, cut very thin slices of the fresh lime that will fit snugly against the walls of the dough shells.

2. If desired, cut out the flesh of the lime slices, leaving just the rind and the fibrous spokes so you can see the curd mixture peeking through.

3. Place the lime slices atop the lime mixture.

4. If desired, sprinkle with zested lime.

Key Lime Tarts

8 mini-cupcakes (see Easy Yellow Cupcakes recipe on page 19), unbaked
1 package ready-made piecrust (contains 2)
½ cup key lime juice (found in produce section)
14 oz (1 can) sweetened condensed milk
3 egg yolks
Green food coloring (optional)

1. Preheat the oven to 350°F and prepare a muffin pan with nonstick spray.

2. Open up the two pie dough sheets. Using a paring knife and a small bowl as a guide, cut four circles of pie dough from each sheet, for a total of eight. Place each dough circle in a cup in the muffin pan, pressing the dough to the sides and bottom. Prick all over with a fork.

3. Bake approximately 15 minutes or just until the edges lightly color. During baking, check several times for bubbles in the dough, and deflate them with a fork. Set the pan aside to cool, leaving the dough shells in their cups.

4. Prepare a mini-cupcake pan with nonstick spray. Follow the cupcake recipe on page 19 but bake a little less time because of the smaller cake size. Set the cakes on a wire rack to cool, and leave the oven on.

5. In a bowl, combine the lime juice, condensed milk, and egg yolks and beat with a whisk until smooth. Since the mixture will actually look lemony rather than bright green, add a few drops of green food coloring, if desired.

6. Place one cooled mini-cupcake in each pastry shell and spoon the lime mixture over it to fill about three-quarters of the shell.

7. Bake for 15 minutes and cool each completed tart on a wire rack.

8. When the tarts are cool, place them in the refrigerator to set, about 1 hour.

Wedding Cupcakes

On display for all the guests to enjoy, each scrumptious lemony cupcake is a symbol of love shared. What a thoughtful idea it would be to give the new couple a copy of the recipes so they can enjoy the sweet memories on all of their anniversaries.

Materials

Lemon Citrus Cupcakes (recipe page 88)

Luscious Buttercream Frosting (recipe page 89)

Fresh blueberries or raspberries

Lemon zest

Orange zest

Design Tip

Fresh fruit and flowers are always lovely decorations on a wedding display. Place them delicately along the tiers so that they look pretty but don't interfere with the cupcakes. To keep the display looking abundant, keep plenty of cakes in the wings and replenish the plates discreetly as the guests take their servings.

Special Tools

Pastry bag with #74 metal tip

Plates and bowls to make the cupcake display tiers

Instructions

1. Fit the tip on the pastry bag and fill the bag with the buttercream icing.

2. Make generous rows of buttercream petals on each cupcake. Hold the pastry bag sideways, as shown in the photo. First pipe the petals around the outer edge of the cake. Start the next row above the edge of the icing of the first row, letting the tip of the petal come up and away from the cupcake. Continue until the cupcake is covered.

3. Place a fresh berry in the center. (It's nice to have different kinds of berries to give variety to the display.) Garnish the top with a light sprinkle of lemon and orange zest.

4. Repeat for all the cupcakes, then arrange them on the tiered display.

Lemon Citrus Cupcakes

2 ½ cups cake flour
2 teaspoons baking powder
½ teaspoon baking soda
¼ teaspoon salt
8 oz (2 sticks) unsalted butter, slightly softened
1 ½ cups granulated sugar
2 large whole eggs, room temperature
3 large egg yolks, room temperature
2 teaspoons vanilla extract
1 teaspoon lemon zest
1 teaspoon orange zest
¼ cup fresh lemon juice
½ cup whole milk

1. Preheat the oven to 350°F. Prepare muffin pans with paper baking cups.

2. In a medium bowl, sift together the flour, baking powder, baking soda, and salt.

3. In the bowl of an electric mixer, beat the butter on medium speed until creamy.

4. Gradually add the sugar, increasing the speed to medium-high and beating until the mixture is light and fluffy (about 3 minutes). Scrape down the sides of the bowl several times during the process.

5. Add the whole eggs and egg yolks, one at a time, beating well after each addition. Beat in the vanilla and lemon and orange zest.

6. Reduce the speed to low and gradually beat in the lemon juice (the batter will appear curdled at this point but will smooth out after you add the dry ingredients).

7. Beat in the dry ingredients in three additions alternately with the milk in two additions. Scrape down the sides of the bowl and beat for another 10 seconds.

8. Fill the prepared cupcake pans. Bake the cupcakes for 18 to 20 minutes, or until a toothpick inserted comes out clean. Cool the cupcakes on a wire rack.

Luscious Buttercream Frosting

1 ¾ cups sugar
½ cup water
6 egg yolks
1 lb (4 sticks) unsalted butter, softened

Special Tools

Candy thermometer

Electric mixer

1. Combine the sugar and water in a medium saucepan and bring to a boil. Boil until a candy thermometer registers 240°F.

2. With an electric mixer, whip the egg yolks until light and fluffy and carefully pour the syrup into the yolks while the mixer is at a moderate speed. Continue whipping until cooled.

3. Add the softened butter in small batches, stopping after each addition.

Wedding Cupcake Displays

You can find wedding cupcake displays in specialty baking shops. If you're planning a small wedding for a family member, consider custom designing the display out of pretty plates and bowls from family members.

In the simple three-tiered design in the photo, a large clear round plate served as the bottom. The middle was a crystal bowl turned upside down with another plate placed safely on top of it; the top was a small pedestal cake plate. When designing a cupcake display, remember to make each tier high enough so that the cupcakes can be easily removed without scraping the frosting.

Red Velvet Cupcakes

You don't have to be a southern belle to make these bright scarlet cakes with snow white frosting—but do rehearse how genteelly you'll accept the lavish compliments.

Materials

24 Red Velvet Cupcakes (recipe at right)

Cream Cheese Frosting (recipe page 21)

Instructions

1. Spread the frosting on the tops of the cupcakes.

2. Display the cupcakes so people can see the intense red color of the cake.

Note: Red velvet cake aficionados divide pretty evenly into two camps: those who use butter and those who use vegetable shortening. Members of the first camp cite butter's intense and wonderful taste and are right when they say it's unbeatable for flavor. But vegetable shortening has nitrogen bubbled into it during processing (to give it that creamy white look), and those bubbles expand during baking to create a cake that is unmistakably lighter and more tender of crumb—a significant attribute in a cake that has "velvet" in its name. Consider trying a recipe with each and decide which one you prefer.

And yes, the recipe really does call for 2 full ounces of red food coloring. Look for large single bottles in your grocery baking section.

Red Velvet Cupcakes

4 oz (1 stick) unsalted butter or shortening, room temperature

1½ cups sugar

2 eggs

2 oz red food coloring

2 tablespoons unsweetened cocoa powder

½ teaspoon salt

1 cup buttermilk

2¼ cups all-purpose flour

1 teaspoon vanilla extract

1 tablespoon distilled white vinegar

1 tablespoon baking soda

1. Preheat the oven to 350°F and prepare the muffin pans with shortening or nonstick spray. Bake without paper cups to get smoother sides.

2. Cream together the butter/shortening and sugar until well blended and light and fluffy.

3. Add the eggs, one at a time, and blend well after each addition.

4. Make a paste with the food coloring and cocoa. Add the paste to the butter/shortening mixture and blend thoroughly.

5. Add the salt and buttermilk to the mixture.

6. Add the flour, vanilla, vinegar, and baking soda in that order, mixing after each addition.

7. Pour the batter into the pans, filling at least halfway. Bake for 15 to 20 minutes, or until a toothpick inserted comes out clean.

8. Remove and turn out the cakes onto a wire rack to cool.

Sweet Memories Cupcakes

Bring back fond memories and form some wonderful new ones with simple candy-topped cupcakes that every age group seems to love. Set out bowls of candy and let young bakers create their own designs.

Materials

24 Easy Yellow Cupcakes (page 19), baked without paper cups for a smooth finish

Classic Buttercream Frosting (page 20)

Candies in colors to harmonize with your frosting colors

Food coloring in your choice of colors

Instructions

1. Plan out your decorating designs in advance since it's difficult to move the candies once they are placed in the frosting.

2. Divide the candies into separate portions so you can quickly select them for each cupcake.

3. Divide the frosting into bowls and tint each a different color. Using a toothpick, add small amounts of color and mix completely until the desired shade is reached.

BAKING TIP: Decorative Touches

Because of their small size, cupcake decorations are often delightfully tiny, the kinds of things you can sprinkle or place with your fingers. They go by the name of jimmies, dragée balls, nonpareils, sprinkles, sparkles, and others. They often come in packets with several different shapes in separate sections, making it easy to add instant charm to a cupcake topping.

Candies are traditional favorites. Adults love simple, specialty candies, the kinds of treats you don't see every day, such as the ones in this project.

Children however, are usually fonder of their favorite movie-matinee brands. Keep a variety of toppings in airtight containers and let the kids mix and match at will.

When you find attractive small candies, buy them in bulk so you always have plenty on hand to make last-minute cupcakes.

Yields 12 cupcakes

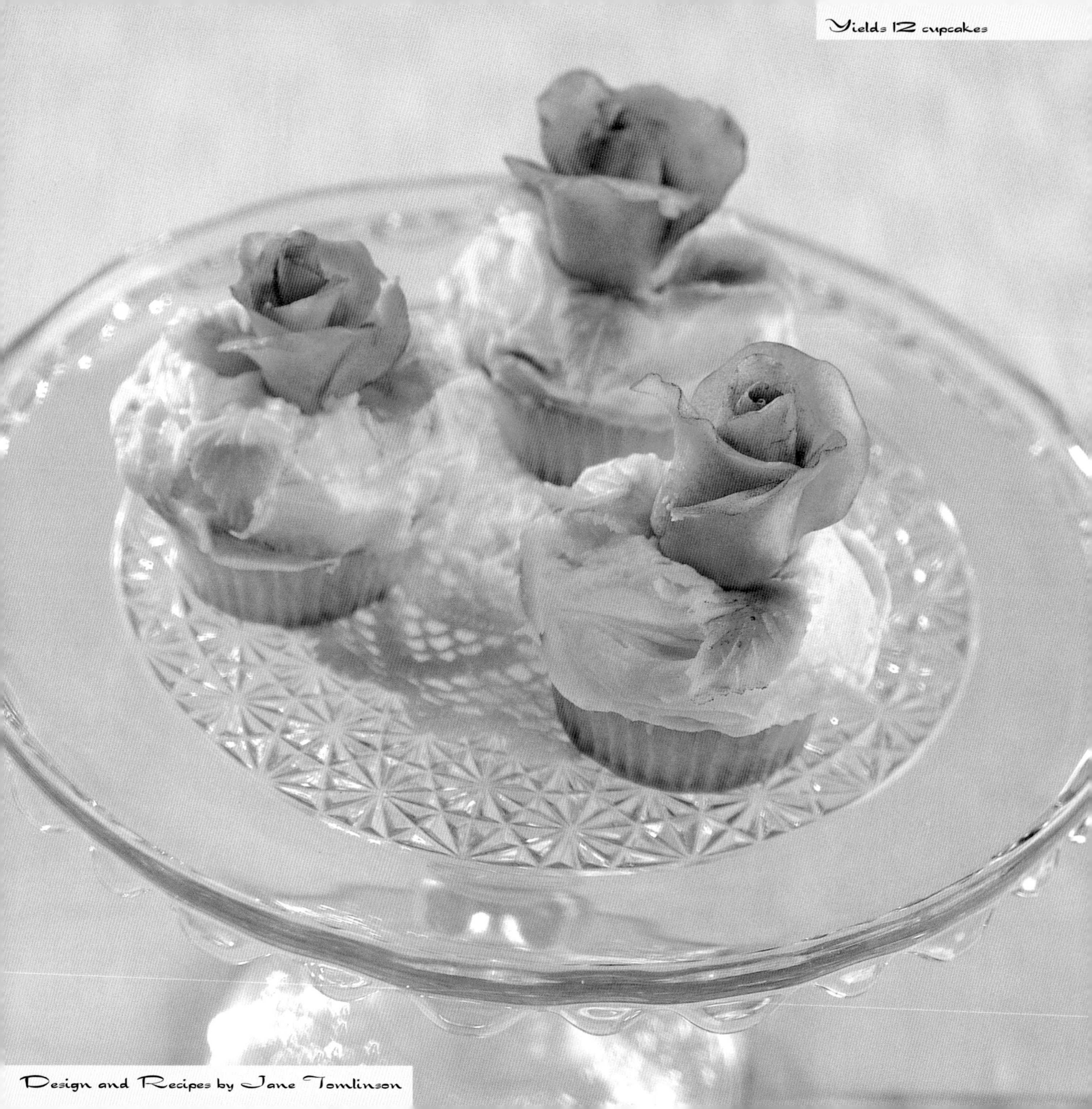

Design and Recipes by Jane Tomlinson

White Chocolate Roses Painted with Petal Dust

These white chocolate flowers are so lifelike, your guests will think they're real. When they find out they are actually chocolate and they're allowed to eat the whole thing—wow!

Materials

12 Classic White or Easy Yellow Cupcakes (recipes pages 18 and 20)

Ivory Buttercream Frosting (recipe page 21)

12 white chocolate roses (recipes pages 95 and 96)

24 to 36 white chocolate leaves (recipe page 95)

Note: Budget enough time to make this project. The white chocolate modeling clay has to set overnight before you can use it. Each rose may be time consuming at first, but once you get the hang of it, you'll be able to work quickly.

Instructions

1. Spread the Ivory Buttercream Frosting on the cupcakes.

2. Place a completed chocolate rose on top of each cake.

3. Arrange the completed leaves around the roses.

White Chocolate Modeling Clay

1 lb white chocolate

⅓ cup light corn syrup

Clear plastic wrap

Special Tools

Double boiler or glass bowl and saucepan

1. Melt the chocolate in a double boiler or glass bowl over simmering water.

2. Remove the bowl when the chocolate is melted, and add the corn syrup.

3. As you stir, and the chocolate cools, the mixture will seize into a ball, similar to children's modeling dough.

4. On a clean surface, knead the ball until the chocolate is smoothly uniform with no unmelted chunks in it.

5. Wrap it tightly in plastic wrap and leave it at room temperature overnight before modeling into roses.

Make the Roses

Materials

White Chocolate Modeling Clay
(recipe page 95)

Toothpicks

1 piece of polystyrene foam,
approximately 1 foot square

Clear plastic wrap

Nylon cel stick (found in baking specialty
stores), or wooden cuticle stick
(found with beauty supplies)

Instructions

Note: The polystyrene foam (available in craft stores) will hold your roses before you place them on the cupcakes, so it should be clean and unused.

1. Take a 1-inch or smaller cube of the chocolate clay and knead it with your hands until it's pliable. Form it into a cone that will become the core of the flower.

2. Place the cone on a toothpick and insert it in the foam.

Repeat 11 times, then allow the cones to harden for about an hour.

3. When the cones have hardened, make the petals. For each petal, take a piece of the chocolate clay, about ½ inch in size, and make a flat disk about the diameter of a nickel (or larger if you're making larger flowers) and about ¼ inch thick. Place the disk between layers of plastic wrap.

4. On a flat surface, or with the disk slightly cupped in the palm of one hand, press with the fingers of the other hand on top of the plastic to thin one side of the disk, shaping the delicate top of the petal. Leave the other side a little thicker, where you'll join it to the base of the core.

5. Remove a core on its toothpick from the foam. Press the thicker side of the petal to the core near the bottom to attach it.

6. Continue to make petals, increasing them gradually in size and layering them, moving upward on the core, until you've reached the size of the flower you desire. Use the photos to guide you. Three petals are sufficient to create a bud; five to seven makes a full rose.

7. Gently shape the petals by pressing their edges with the cel stick or cuticle stick.

8. Place the rose, still on its toothpick, back into the foam. Continue until you have made a rose for each cupcake, and let the flowers dry overnight.

Dark Chocolate Modeling Clay

1 lb good quality semisweet chocolate

(don't use chips)

½ cup light corn syrup

Clear plastic wrap

Special Tools

Double boiler or glass bowl and saucepan

1. Follow the directions for the White Chocolate Modeling Clay on page 95.

Paint the Roses

Materials

White Chocolate roses

Petal dust in colors of roses (found in bakery specialty stores)

Instructions

1. Touch the tip of your paint-brush with a tiny amount of petal dust. Dip the paintbrush between the petals to dust them with color.

2. Using the side of the tip, dust the edges of the petals.

Make the Leaves

Materials

White Chocolate Modeling Clay (recipe page 95)

Toothpicks

Clear plastic wrap

Petal dust in moss green

Special Tools

Leaf-shaped cutter

Veining tool (optional)

Small paintbrush

Instructions

1. Take a 1-inch cube of the chocolate clay and warm it with your hands, then use a rolling pin to roll it out into a circle about ⅛ inch thick.

2. Use a leaf-shaped cutter to cut out the leaf.

3. Use a toothpick or a cake decorator's veining tool to draw the veins.

4. Let the leaf dry over crumpled plastic wrap. Brush it with the green petal dust. Repeat for the number of leaves you want. Two or three leaves per flower looks best.

Design and Recipes by Rose Reitzel-Perry

Truffle Surprise Cupcakes

It seems so innocent, this delicate raspberry-colored cake. But bite into it, and what a wicked little surprise you find inside! Hand-made chocolate truffles are the secret. The trick is to keep them from melting. Read on.

Materials

16 Chocolate Truffles (recipe page 100)

16 Classic White Cupcakes (recipe page 18), unbaked

Raspberry Buttercream Frosting (recipe at right)

Special Tools

Pastry bag with tiny round tip

Before You Start

If desired, make your pastry bag from parchment paper. (See instructions on page 101.) Cut a tiny hole in the end of it.

Instructions

1. Make the truffles according to the Chocolate Truffles recipe on page 100, keeping the leftover chocolate warm to use for decorating. It's very important to put the truffles in the freezer as soon as they are prepared and keep them there while you make the cakes.

2. Preheat the oven to 350°F and prepare the muffin pans with white or pastel paper cups for 16 cupcakes.

3. Fill the cups slightly less than halfway with the cake batter, reserving the rest.

4. Bake 10 minutes, then remove from the oven.

5. Center a frozen truffle on each cupcake. If, by the time you've placed them all, the first truffles are still sitting on top of their cakes, give them a little nudge down so the tops of the truffles are flush with the tops of the cakes.

6. Top each truffle with a tea-spoon of the reserved cake batter, and return the cupcakes to the oven for another 10 minutes, or until a toothpick inserted in the cake part comes out clean.

7. Invert the warm cupcakes onto a cooling rack, and let them cool upside down.

8. When the cupcakes are thoroughly cooled, turn then right side up. Spread the tops with the Raspberry Buttercream Frosting, making it smooth and even.

9. The reserved chocolate should be liquid, but if it isn't, put it back over simmering water in the double boiler for a couple minutes. Spoon the chocolate into the pastry bag.

10. Line up the cupcakes and pipe several parallel stripes on them. (Use the photo to guide you.)

Raspberry Buttercream Frosting

Note: If you can't find raspberry purée at the grocery store, make it by pressing ½ cup fresh or thawed frozen raspberries through a sieve and discarding the seeds.

¼ cup raspberry purée
2 cups Classic Buttercream Frosting (recipe page 20)
1 to 2 tablespoons raspberry liqueur (optional)

1. Whip the raspberry purée into the Buttercream Frosting.

2. If desired, add the raspberry liqueur.

Chocolate Truffles

3 tablespoons heavy cream

1 tablespoon raspberry liqueur

4 oz chocolate bar, broken into dime-size pieces

(use high quality semisweet chocolate)

Special Tools

Double boiler (or bowl over a saucepan)

Melon baller

1. In the double boiler–over simmering (not boiling) water–combine all the ingredients. Stir over the heat until the mixture is completely smooth. It helps to taste at this point, because your tongue can detect slight graininess that your eyes may not see. Don't be tempted to add extra liqueur; it will make it too sticky.

2. When the chocolate has reached the desired smoothness, remove the pan from the heat and put it in the freezer for 15 minutes or in the refrigerator for an hour, until it has solidified to a fudgy consistency.

3. Use the melon baller to make the 16 small truffles, ½ to ¾ inch in diameter. If you don't have a melon baller, use the tip of a spoon to portion out the chocolate, and roll it between your palms to form spheres. If the heat from your hands makes this sloppy work, return the chocolate to the freezer for a few minutes.

4. Put the truffles in the freezer while you make the cake. Don't wash the chocolate pan yet. Place it on top of the stove so that the heat of the oven will liquefy it for later decorating.

Design Tip

If you've never piped chocolate before, practice on a clean plate until you get the hang of it. Keep your wrist stiff, hold your elbow against your body, use your other hand to brace your arm, and make the movement with your whole body. If you go too slowly, you'll get a wavy line; too fast, you'll get a broken line. Practice chocolate can be scraped off the plate, put back into the pot and melted again.

BAKING TIP:

Make Your Own Pastry Bag

You can buy decorating pastry bag kits with a selection of tips. They contain sturdy reusable bags that you wash after each use. If you're making a lot of different frosting colors with simple piping of small or straight shapes, you'll save washing time by making your own pastry bags out of parchment paper. Here's how.

1. Make a double-layered pastry bag from a rectangle of parchment paper that is about 8 x 10 inches. (Don't substitute waxed paper—it will melt when you're using hot ingredients.)

2. Fold the rectangle in half to form a triangle.

3. With the top of the triangle pointing away from you, roll the left corner of the paper toward the center of the triangle, forming a cone. Pull the corner upward until it meets the top point of the triangle and forms a tight tip at the bottom of the cone.

4. Repeat this action with the right side of the triangle, rolling it around the back of your cone until it touches the top of the triangle and forms a tight tip.

5. To hold the cone together, fold the top and tips of the pastry bag toward you and the center of the bag, making a sturdy cuff.

6. With scissors make a very small hole at the bottom of the cone, about the size of a pinhead, to serve as your pastry bag tip.

Maple Walnut Streusel Cupcakes

Even if you're not in a chalet overlooking the Bavarian Alps, this streusel cupcake is most appetizing. It's perfect for Sunday brunches or business meetings, when guests love tasty treats without sugary tops.

Materials

Maple Streusel Topping (recipe at right)

12 Maple Walnut Cupcakes (recipe far right), unbaked

Instructions

1. Prepare and bake the streusel topping.

2. Pour the cupcake batter into a muffin pan prepared with paper baking cups, and fill them three-quarters.

3. Cover each filled cup with the streusel mixture.

4. Bake until the cakes are bouncy in the middle, 15 to 20 minutes. Set on a wire rack to cool before serving.

Maple Streusel Topping

1 oz brown sugar
3 tablespoons unsalted butter, room temperature
2 tablespoons pure maple syrup
2½ oz all-purpose flour
2 oz chopped walnuts

Special Tools

mixer with a paddle attachment

1. Preheat the oven to 350°F. In the bowl of the electric mixer, cream the brown sugar with the butter. When the mixture has softened, add the maple syrup, keeping the mixer running until it's incorporated. Add the flour and mix it in, then add the walnuts.

2. Spread the mixture onto a baking sheet and bake for 6 to 8 minutes, until it browns lightly. Let it cool. It will be like a hard cookie, so use a dough cutter or sharp knife to crumble it up, then set the mixture aside.

Maple Walnut Cupcakes

7½ oz flour
5 oz brown sugar
1½ teaspoons baking powder
½ teaspoon salt
4 oz (1 stick) unsalted butter, room temperature
2 eggs
¼ cup pure maple syrup
¼ cup milk
1 cup chopped walnuts

Special Tools

Electric mixer with a paddle attachment

1. Turn the oven down or preheat it to 325°F after you've made the streusel topping, and prepare a muffin pan with paper baking cups.

2. Place the first four ingredients into the bowl of an electric mixer with paddle blade.

3. Cut in the butter, and beat until combined.

4. Add the eggs, maple syrup, and milk.

5. Once mixed, add the walnuts.

Yields 24 cupcakes

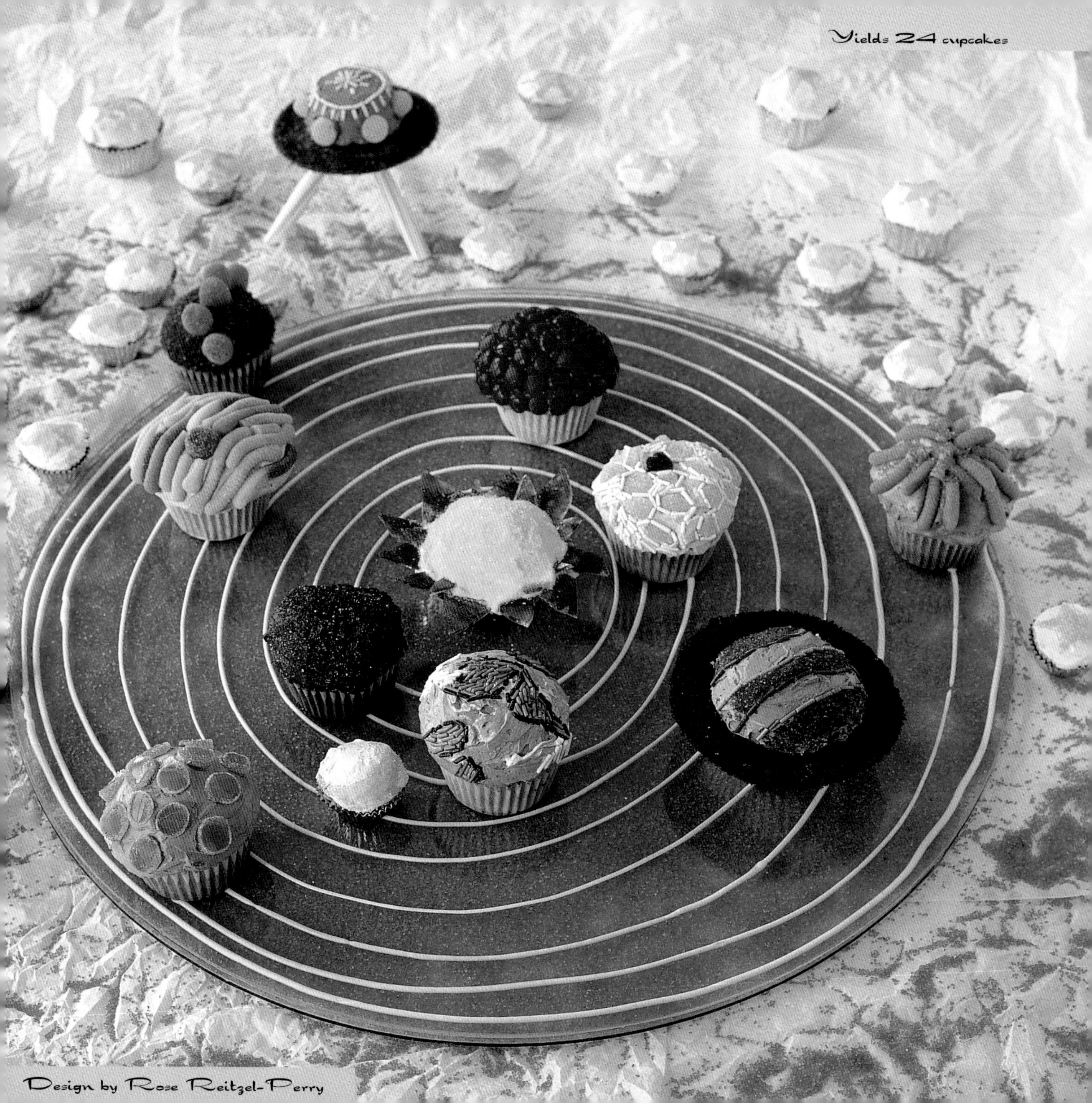

Design by Rose Reitzel-Perry

Cupcake Solar System

The big question is—what's more fun, making this completely edible cosmic creation? Or watching everyone enjoy it?

Materials

11 regular size cupcakes for the sun, nine planets, and the UFO (see the Easy Yellow Cupcakes recipe on page 19) and as many regular size or mini-cupcakes for the stars as you want, baked in gold foil cups if you wish

Classic Buttercream Frosting (see recipe on page 20)

Royal Icing (see recipe on page 65)

3 or 4 or more small containers

Edible white cake glitter (optional)

Sanding sugars in yellow, red, white, purple, green, blue, and silver (found in specialty baking stores)

Food coloring in yellow, red, blue, green, and black

Candies:

Sugar fruit rings in red, yellow, and orange

Gumdrops in orange, red, green, and purple

Cinnamon candies

Cylindrical sprinkles or jimmies

Sour candy worms

Candy sticks or cookie sticks such as hazelnut crème wafers

Parchment paper

2 round pieces of clear glass, about 20 inches in diameter

Marking paper, such as brown paper

Special Tools

Star-shaped cookie cutter (optional)

Round cookie or biscuit cutter, about 3 inches in diameter

Silicone mat or light-colored baking sheet

Scissors

Tweezers

Paper cone or pastry bag with small round tip

Pastry brush

Before You Start

1. Bake all your cupcakes and let them cool. Make the Buttercream Frosting and store it in a bowl in your work area.

2. Make star-shaped stencils for whatever size(s) you want your star cupcakes to be. (See instructions for making stencils in the Winter Spice Cupcakes project on page 53.) Or use a star-shaped cookie cutter. If you like, make a crescent moon stencil for a mini-cupcake moon to go with the Earth.

3. Since they require careful watching, make the sugar parts for the Sun and Saturn and the UFO ahead of time and set them aside until needed. See instructions on page 106.

105

4. Create a small area just for sugaring the tops of the cupcakes, where you have handy the containers of colored sanding sugar and several cooling racks placed over parchment paper. When you've frosted a cupcake, place it on a cooling rack and really douse it with the sugar. Shake the excess off the cupcake, then fold the paper into a funnel to put the extra sugar back in its container.

5. If desired, make as many parchment paper pastry bags as you'll need.(See instructions on page 101.)

6. Lay out all your materials and tools. Follow our suggestions in the steps below if you wish, but feel free to decorate the heavenly bodies any way you like. Especially if you have young helpers on your creative team, keep handy enough small bowls or containers to allow for out-of-this-world frosting color combinations.

7. As a general rule, 1½ tablespoons makes a portion of frosting for each of the regular size cupcakes; you'll use less, of course for the mini-cupcakes.

Use about half the white frosting to cover the mini-cupcake stars.

Out of the remaining white buttercream:

• Save a little to make ocean wave peaks for Earth.

• Dye 1 portion red to spread on Mars.

• Dye 2 portions yellow. Use 1 for the sun. To the other, add a little red to make yellow orange for Jupiter.

• Use the rest to make the cool colors such as blue, green, aqua and purple for the remaining planets.

Design Tip

This project was designed as a display for children, with bold, cheery colors and familiar matinee-movie candies. To make an elegant adult version, subdue all the decorations, and use black or silver (which is a shiny black) sanding sugar instead of blue.

Planetary Orbits

Starting from the sun, the planets should be placed in this order:

Mercury
Venus
Earth
Mars
Jupiter
Saturn
Uranus
Neptune
Pluto

Instructions: Make the Melted Sugar Parts

The Sun's Rays

1. Melt red, yellow, and orange sugar fruit rings in a 300°F oven on a silicone mat or a well-oiled light-colored baking sheet. (It's hard to see melting sugar on a dark surface.) Melting time is between 3 and 7 minutes usually, but you must watch the candies carefully because once they reach the melt stage they can burn if you don't remove them quickly.

2. Let the candy puddles cool, then break them into shards. (See photo, opposite page at bottom.)

Saturn's Rings

1. Place the round cookie cutter on a silicone mat or well-oiled nonstick baking sheet. Sprinkle an even ⅛ to ¼ inch of sanding sugar (we used red, but any color(s) is fine) inside the cutter, and put it in a 300°F oven. If you want, you can make the UFO ring at the same time.

2. Leave the oven door cracked so you can watch it carefully for 3 to 7 minutes so the sugar doesn't burn and make a mess. Once the entire surface of the sugar looks wet, pull it from the oven, remove the cookie cutter, and let the sugar circle cool. (See photo on page 108.)

UFO Ring

1. Use the same techniques you used to make Saturn's rings, but use green sanding sugar sprinkled with a little blue, and make it at least ¼ inch thick, because it's load bearing. (See photo on page 109.)

Instructions: Make the Stars

1. Frost the mini-cupcakes with the white Buttercream Frosting. If you like, add an extra sheen by sprinkling edible white cake glitter over the frosting.

2. Hold a stencil over each cupcake, and sprinkle colored sanding sugar over it. We used yellow, but you can use any color(s) you wish. Be sure to lift the stencil off carefully to avoid spilling sugar where you don't want it.

Instructions: Make the Sun

1. Spread yellow frosting on the cupcake and douse it with yellow sanding sugar.

2. Stick the sugar candy shards into the cupcake so they look like solar rays.

Instructions:
Make the Planets

Uranus

Spread orange frosting on the cupcake. With the scissors, cut polka dots from orange gumdrops and arrange the dots on the frosting.

Mars

Spread red buttercream on the cupcake. Dot the top with hot cinnamon candies (it's the angry red planet, after all) and sprinkle it with red sanding sugar.

Jupiter

Spread yellow-orange frosting on the cupcake. Stick on a red gumdrop for Jupiter's red spot (the eye of the storms constantly raging across the planet). Cut the candy worms to the right length and arrange them in stripes across the surface.

Neptune

Spread blue frosting on the cupcake. Use scissors to cut off the blue part of some candy worms. Arrange them like the seaweed dreadlocks of Neptune, god of the ocean.

Earth

Add some plain white frosting to blue but don't mix them. Frost the cupcake with the unmixed blend to get a swirly, ocean wave effect. (See the photo to guide you.) Use tweezers to draw continents with brown, white, and green sprinkles. Since Earth is your home, decorate it with anything you want.

Venus

Spread aqua frosting on the cupcake. Cut a heart (for Venus, the goddess of love) from a red gumdrop. With tweezers, arrange white sprinkles between the gumdrops to represent clouds of ammonia. Or just sprinkle with white sanding sugar.

Saturn

1. With a serrated knife, slice off the top of the cupcake and eat it. Spread a little green frosting on top of the bottom flat piece and completely cover the top piece. Set the two pieces aside for now.

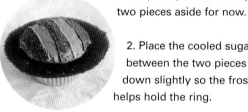

2. Place the cooled sugar Saturn ring in between the two pieces of cake. Press down slightly so the frosting in the center helps hold the ring.

3. On the top of the cake, make stripes with bands of colored sanding sugar. (See page 71 for tips on making sugar stripes.) Outline the stripes with sprinkles.

Pluto

Spread purple frosting on the cupcake. Decorate with purple gumdrops and purple sanding sugar. Pluto is so weird, some astronomers don't even think it's a real planet—make it look spooky.

Mercury

Make this one last, because you can combine all the leftover colors of frosting, and add a drop of black food coloring to make black frosting. Mercury looks all burnt up because it's closest to the sun. Cover the top with silver sanding sugar, which comes out looking black anyway.

Instructions: Make the UFO

1. Use Royal Icing like glue to attach candy sticks to the bottom of the sugar circle you made. You'll have to prop up the construction for several hours while the icing dries (small jars or cans or pieces of polystyrene foam will work), but make sure the props can be removed.

2. Slice off the top of the cupcake and eat it. Turn the bottom upside down and spread it with green frosting. Decorate with sprinkles and portholes made of gumdrops.

3. Once the legs are firmly glued on, turn the saucer right side up and use Royal Icing to glue the top on. The UFO is pretty delicate, so handle it carefully.

Instructions: Make the Solar System Display

1. Clean and thoroughly dry the two circles of glass.

2. Place one of the glass circles on top of the marking paper and trace its circumference on the paper, then set the glass aside. Now draw on the paper the nine orbit lines of the solar system. Don't worry about scientific accuracy–make the lines as close or as far apart as you want. Make them round rather than elliptical.

3. Put the glass back on the paper. Pipe the orbit lines with the Royal Icing. Start the orbits from the middle, so that if you mess up you can wipe it away without ruining the other lines. (Don't throw away the marked paper. Keep it for the next galaxy you make.)

4. To create the color under the orbits, sprinkle a generous amount of blue sanding sugar on the other piece of glass. Don't worry if there are any bare spots, just try to cover them up the best you can–a dry pastry brush works well. Place the glass with the orbits carefully over the sugar-covered bottom piece.

5. Carry the sandwiched glass pieces carefully to the display area and set them down. Place the sun in the center, then set the planets on their orbits. (See the Planetary Orbits chart on page 106.) At the last minute, set out the UFO as if it's just entering the solar system from a galaxy far, far away.

Design and Glaze Recipe by Emma Pearson

Harvest Basket with Pumpkin Spice Cakes

Nestle glowing pumpkin-spice cupcakes in a basket made of real chocolate leaves—your guests won't stop thanking you!

Materials

24 Pumpkin Spice Cupcakes (recipe page 113), still warm

Maple Orange Glaze (recipe page 112), still warm

For One Chocolate Leaf Basket:

6 oz each of milk chocolate chips, dark chocolate chips, and butterscotch chips

About 15 sturdy, nontoxic leaves of different varieties (such as baby kale, spinach, or rose geranium), ranging from ½ to 2 inches long and about 1 inch wide

Parchment paper

Baking sheet

Waxed paper

Small artist's paintbrush

Shallow pie dish

Clear plastic wrap

Silver petal dust (found in specialty baking stores)

Special Tools

Double boiler or heat-resistant glass bowl and saucepan

Instructions: Make the Chocolate Leaves

1. Melt the milk chocolate chips in the top of the double boiler.

2. While the chocolate is melting, lay out a piece of the parchment paper on the baking sheet. Have small pieces of waxed paper nearby.

3. Wash and dry the leaves and lay one-third of them flat on the parchment paper, with space between them.

4. When the chocolate has melted, remove ¼ cup of it and set it aside. Using the chocolate in the pan, place about 1 teaspoon of chocolate onto one of the leaves. With the paintbrush, spread the chocolate to coat this side of the leaf, covering it completely. It should be about ⅛ inch thick, solid enough to cool into a shape it will keep, and thin enough to take on the texture of the leaf. Make sure the chocolate does not spread onto the opposite side of the leaf.

5. Place the coated leaf on a sheet of waxed paper and put it in the refrigerator for about 3 to 4 minutes, until chilled so the chocolate is solid.

6. Remove the leaf from the refrigerator and peel the real leaf away from the chocolate. Keep the chocolate leaf in a cool place.

7. Repeat for all the leaves in this batch until the milk chocolate is used up. You may reuse any leaves that are sturdy enough for a second coating.

8. Clean the bowl or pan and melt the dark chocolate chips and repeat steps 4 to 7, using half the remaining leaves.

9. Repeat steps 4 to 7 with the butterscotch chips, using the last batch of leaves. Store the finished candy leaves in a cool place, such as in a covered container in the refrigerator, until you are ready to assemble the basket.

Instructions:
Assemble the Basket

1. Use the pie dish as a mold to guide the shaping of your basket and hold it as you're working. Line the dish with clear plastic wrap–when the basket is completed, you can easily lift it out of the dish.

2. Remelt the ¼ cup of chocolate you set aside in step 4 when making the leaves on previous page. While the chocolate is melting, place a serving dish in the refrigerator to chill.

3. Dip the paintbrush into the melted chocolate and paint an area on the back of one leaf and the front of another where you can join them.

4. Gently press them together. As the chocolate cools and hardens, it will hold the leaves together.

5. Repeat, mixing the different leaf colors and shapes as you desire. Use the photo to guide you.

6. When you've finished the basket, you may paint a small area of each leaf with the silver petal dust to give it a frosty look.

7. Use a wide spatula and your hands to gently move the basket to its chilled display plate. Be very gentle with the basket, and when you place it on the table, keep it away from warm foods–the connection between the leaves is fragile, and you don't want the chocolate to melt again.

8. Gently place three or four completely cooled cupcakes inside the basket. Top them with chocolate leaves if you wish.

9. Arrange the remaining cupcakes around the basket.

Maple Orange Glaze

6 tablespoons maple syrup

4 tablespoons fresh squeezed orange juice

2 tablespoon brown sugar

Grated piece of orange peel

Edible white cake glitter (optional)

1. Combine all the ingredients in a saucepan and heat until the sugar has dissolved.

2. Keep the glaze warm until ready to use. If the glaze cools before the cakes are ready, you may reheat it gently.

3. Pour the warm glaze over the cupcakes, letting any excess glaze fall on the parchment paper below the cooling rack.

4. If you like, sprinkle the glitter on the warm glaze. It will melt and give the glaze a lovely sheen.

Design Tip

Since the connection between the leaves is fragile, it's better to make several small baskets than try to make one big one. Use white chocolate to make a summery basket.

Time-Saving Tip

For a square or rectangular basket, make upright sides like a short fence, using a pretty display plate as the bottom of the basket.

Pumpkin Spice Cupcakes

2 cups sifted cake flour

1 teaspoon baking soda

¼ teaspoon baking powder

½ teaspoon salt

½ teaspoon ground cardamom

½ teaspoon ground ginger

¼ teaspoon ground nutmeg

4 oz (1 stick) unsalted butter, room temperature

1½ cups brown sugar

2 eggs

1 cup pumpkin purée

1 teaspoon vanilla extract

½ cup buttermilk

1. Preheat the oven to 350°F and prepare muffin pans with nonstick spray or paper cups.

2. Resift the sifted cake flour with the baking soda, baking powder, salt, and spices.

3. Cream the butter and sugar until fluffy.

4. Add the eggs to the butter mixture one at a time, mixing well after each. Add the pumpkin purée and vanilla and beat to incorporate.

5. Alternating the dry ingredients with the buttermilk, blend half of one, then the other into the butter mixture. Mix well after each addition and repeat. Mix until well blended.

6. Pour the batter into the pans, filling at least halfway. Bake for 20 to 25 minutes, until the cakes test done.

7. Remove the pans and turn out the cupcakes onto a wire rack placed over parchment to cool.

Design and Icing Recipe by Martha Vining

Lemon Meringue Cupcakes

Nothing quite matches the sweet-sour zest of lemon meringue pie—unless it's a luscious cupcake version, crowned with perfect peaks of toasted meringue.

Before You Start

For this recipe you'll be using a handheld mixer while you keep the meringue icing warm on the stove, so make sure your mixer can be used safely in that location. You'll also want to have at least a small work area right next to the stove so you can continue mixing the ingredients after removing the mixing bowl from the stove.

Materials

12 Classic Lemon Cupcakes (recipe page 116)

Fluffy White Icing (recipe page 117)

1 cup lemon curd (found with jellies and jams in grocery stores)

Special Tools

Handheld culinary torch (found in specialty cooking or hardware stores)

Instructions

1. Using a serrated knife, slice each cooled cupcake in the middle horizontally. Spread 1 tablespoon of the lemon curd on top of the bottom half. Replace the top of the cupcake, capturing the lemon curd in the middle.

2. Using a small metal spatula, completely cover the sides and top of each cupcake with the Fluffy White Icing. Use a gentle upswing movement to form small peaks all over the sides and top.

3. Follow the manufacturer's instructions on the torch and lightly brown the icing peaks, browning a bit more on the top than on the sides. It might take you a few tries to learn the exact touch to give the flame on the torch–if you burn some of the icing, just remove it with a fork and then smooth and peak the icing and try again.

Design Tip

A handheld culinary torch operates somewhat like a crafter's glue gun. You'll find all kinds of uses for the torch in your kitchen, such as making crème brûlée, finishing the cheese on onion soup gratiné or huevos rancheros, or adding attractive and tasty browning to any number of microwaved dishes. You can even toast marshmallows with it.

Time-Saving Tip

If you don't have a culinary torch, you can brown the tops of meringue peaks by placing the cupcakes under the broiler for a few minutes. It won't have the same artistic effect as using the torch on each cupcake, but it won't take as long either.

115

Classic Lemon Cupcakes

1 ¾ cups sifted cake flour

2 teaspoons baking powder

¼ teaspoon salt

¾ cup milk

2 teaspoons lemon extract

1¼ cups sugar

4 oz (1 stick) unsalted butter, room temperature

3 egg whites

1. Preheat the oven to 350°F and prepare muffin pans with nonstick spray and flour.

2. Resift the sifted cake flour with the baking powder and salt.

3. Combine the milk and lemon extract.

4. Cream the sugar and butter until fluffy.

5. Alternating the flour mixture with the milk mixture, blend half of one, then the other into the butter mixture. Mix well after each addition and repeat. Mix until well blended.

6. In a separate bowl, beat the egg whites until stiff, but not dry. Fold them into the batter.

7. Pour the batter into the muffin pans, filling at least halfway. Bake for 15 to 20 minutes, until the cakes test done.

8. Remove the pans and turn out the cupcakes onto a wire rack to cool.

9. Use half the cupcakes for this project and save the rest for another.

Yields 24 cupcakes

Fluffy White Icing

2 egg whites

1½ cups sugar

⅓ cup water

¼ teaspoon cream of tartar

Special Tools

**Double boiler or heat-resistant
mixing bowl over pan on stove**

Handheld electric mixer

1. Combine all the ingredients in the top pan of a double boiler or in a medium, heat-resistant mixing bowl placed over a pan of boiling water. Keep the heat or flame low on the stove. (To create the high peaks, you want to keep the temperature of the mixture consistently warm.)

2. Beat the mixture with the electric mixer on medium speed until it's light and fluffy. (Ordinarily you don't use your mixer while the mixing bowl is still on the stove, so be sure you keep the mixer's electric cord away from heating elements.)

3. Remove the bowl from the heat, and continue beating the mixture until it's cool.

Yields enough for 12 cupcakes

Design and Recipes by Emma Pearson
Alternate Recipes by Veronika Alice Gunter

Vegan Musical Notes

You'll savor sweet, natural notes with these pretty cupcakes that are made without any animal products. We've provided two sets of recipes—one for the purist vegan who keeps specialty ingredients in the pantry, and another for the vegan in a hurry. Both are delicious.

Materials

18 Purist Vegan Chocolate Marble Cupcakes (page 120) and Tofu & Maple Vegan Frosting (page 120)

or

12 Easy Vegan Chocolate Marble Cupcakes (page 121)

Easy Vegan Frosting (page 121)

Parchment paper

Marking pen

10 oz dark chocolate chips, plus extra for garnish

Silver petal dust (optional)

Special Tools

Pastry bag with tiny round tip

Before You Start

1. If desired, make your pastry bag from parchment paper. (See instructions on page 101.) Cut a tiny hole in the end of it.

2. Use a marking pen to draw musical notes and symbols, about 1 to 1½ inches high, on a sheet of parchment paper. Make sure you can clearly see the shapes through the other side of the parchment paper. Then turn the paper over, so the marks are now on the underside of the paper, and lay it on a flat surface.

Instructions

1. Melt the chocolate in a double boiler or a bowl over a pan of hot water. Spoon the chocolate into the pastry bag.

2. Working quickly while the chocolate is still warm, gently squeeze the chocolate onto the shapes seen through the parchment paper. (Practice a little first on a scrap piece of parchment paper, so you become familiar with the feel of it.)

3. Carefully place the parchment paper with the notes into the freezer for 2 to 3 minutes or until hardened. Keep frozen until you're ready to use them.

4. With a free, swirling motion, spread the frosting on top of the cooled cupcakes.

5. Remove the hardened shapes from the freezer. Peel them gently from the parchment paper. If you like, lightly dust the flat side, which is now the front side, of the shapes with the silver petal dust.

6. Arrange the shapes on the frosting, angled so the silver sides face upward.

7. Decorate the display plate with more dark chocolate chips.

Design Tips for Vegan Chocolate Lovers

Dark chocolate (also called bittersweet, semisweet, or sweet chocolate) is often—but not always—vegan. By definition, dark chocolate consists of 15 to 35 percent chocolate solids, plus sugar, cocoa butter, and vanilla. However, certain dark chocolates can contain up to 12 percent milk, so read the labels carefully.

119

18 Purist Vegan Chocolate Marble Cupcakes

1 ½ cups maple syrup

¾ cup safflower oil

4 ½ oz firm tofu

½ cup water

2 tablespoons pure vanilla extract

3 cups spelt flour
(available at whole food grocers)

2 teaspoons nonaluminum baking powder

1 teaspoon baking soda

1 teaspoon fine sea salt

¾ cup chocolate powder

1. Preheat the oven to 350°F and prepare muffin pans with shortening or oil and flour.

2. In a blender, combine the maple syrup, oil, tofu, water, and vanilla and blend until smooth.

3. In a large bowl, whisk together the flour, baking powder, baking soda, and salt. Add the wet mixture, using as few strokes as possible.

4. Place one-third of the mixture in a separate bowl and blend in the chocolate powder. Pour the chocolate mixture into the lighter mixture and, using a fork, lightly combine with only a few strokes, leaving a marbled effect.

5. Spoon the batter carefully into the muffin pans, and bake for 15 to 20 minutes or until a toothpick inserted comes out clean. Turn out the cupcakes and cool them on a wire rack.

Tofu and Maple Vegan Frosting

1 lb tofu

½ cup maple syrup

¼ cup tahini

2 tablespoons chocolate powder

2 teaspoons vanilla extract

Put all ingredients into a blender and blend until smooth.

12 Easy Vegan Chocolate Marble Cupcakes

1½ cups unbleached all-purpose white flour

1 cup milled cane sugar or white sugar

1 teaspoon baking soda

½ teaspoon salt

1 cup cold water (for mocha flavor, substitute ½ cup water plus ½ cup cold coffee)

6 tablespoons safflower or vegetable oil

1 teaspoon vanilla extract

2 tablespoons white vinegar

½ cup unsweetened cocoa powder

1. Preheat the oven to 350°F and prepare a muffin pan with shortening or oil and flour.

2. In a medium bowl, combine the flour, sugar, baking soda, and salt, mixing well.

3. In a large separate bowl, combine the water, oil, and vanilla.

4. Gradually add the dry ingredients to the liquid, mixing as you do, until the batter is smooth.

5. Add the vinegar, stirring quickly and thoroughly. (The white color you see is a sign of the reaction of the baking soda and the vinegar. It won't be visible in the finished cupcakes.)

6. Place one-third of the mixture in a separate bowl and blend in the cocoa powder. Pour the chocolate mixture into the lighter mixture and, using a fork, lightly combine with only a few strokes, leaving a marbled effect.

7. Spoon the batter carefully into the muffin pan, and bake for 15 to 20 minutes or until a toothpick inserted comes out clean. Turn out the cupcakes and cool them on a wire rack.

Easy Vegan Frosting

1 cup milled cane sugar or white sugar

6 tablespoons cornstarch

4 tablespoons cocoa powder

½ teaspoon salt

1 cup water

2 tablespoons safflower or vegetable oil

½ teaspoon vanilla extract

1. Mix the dry ingredients in a medium saucepan. Whisk in the water. Heat over medium heat to thicken, continuing to whisk as you do. The mixture may thicken quickly or take a minute or so at boiling to come to a thickness good for spreading. As soon as it reaches that thickness, remove it from the heat.

2. Stir in the oil and vanilla. Cool and set aside until ready to use.

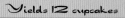

Design and Recipes by Rose Reitzel-Perry

Silver Solstice Sparklers

Put away your megaphone. The starburst buttercream frosting makes the announcement loud and clear—the party's on!

Materials

12 chocolate cupcakes baked in silver foil baking cups (see Chocolate Buttermilk Cupcake on page 19 or use a favorite fudgy recipe of your own)

Chocolate Glaze (recipe page 125)

Flavored Buttercream Frosting (recipe page 124)

White coarse sugar (found in specialty baking stores)

Silver-coated almonds (found in specialty baking stores)

12 candles or sparklers

Special Tools

Pastry bag with a small star tip

Instructions

1. Using a spoon, carefully cover the tops of the cakes with the Chocolate Glaze. Alternatively, dip the tops of the cupcakes in the bowl–as you pull up, give the cupcake a little shake and roll your wrist as you turn it right side up to keep the glaze from running down the sides.

2. The glaze should cool before you top it with the frosting. The glaze dries fairly quickly at room temperature, so the first glazed cake will probably be ready to frost by the time the last one is glazed. Check by lightly touching it; it should be solid, but if you do leave a faint fingerprint, the frosting will hide it.

3. Fill the pastry bag with the Flavored Buttercream Frosting. You might find it more comfortable to work with a half-full bag, and refill as you go along.

4. Pipe the buttercream in peaks, starting in the middle of each cupcake and working to the edges. Don't worry about putting on too much frosting–it's so light it won't overwhelm the cake, even if you're overgenerous.

5. Sprinkle white coarse sugar onto the finished cupcakes to give them an extra festive sparkle.

6. Display the cakes on a bed of white coarse sugar and silver-coated almonds.

7. To avoid spilling wax or dropping burnt matches into the frosting, light the candles first, then place them into the cupcakes. Bring the cakes to the table with sparklers already ablaze.

Design Tip

Practice peaking the buttercream frosting on a clean plate until you get your technique down. You can mix your practice buttercream back into the main batch.

Flavored Buttercream Frosting

3 egg whites

½ cup sugar

¼ cup corn syrup

10 oz (2½ sticks) unsalted butter, room temperature

1 teaspoon flavored extract or 1 tablespoon clear liqueur, such as
triple sec or white crème de menthe

Special Tools

Electric mixer

1. With the electric mixer, whip the egg whites until they're frothy.

2. Stir together the sugar and corn syrup in a heavy saucepan until evenly moist. Put the pan over medium-high heat, and don't stir it anymore, but watch it. When the surface is covered with little bubbles, remove it from the heat.

3. Now you have to act quickly. If you have a standing mixer, turn it on low-medium and carefully add the hot syrup to the egg whites, pouring close to the edge of the bowl so it won't splash back at you.

If you have a hand mixer, add the syrup in three stages, whipping between additions. Remember, the hot sugar can really burn— don't let it touch your skin. Once all the syrup is added, increase the speed of the mixer, and whip until the outside of the bowl is cool.

4. With the mixer at medium speed, gradually add the soft butter, about a tablespoon at a time.

5. On low speed, drizzle in the flavoring of your choice.

Chocolate Glaze

4 oz good quality semisweet
chocolate

⅓ cup heavy cream

Special Tools

Double boiler

1. Break the chocolate into
dime-size pieces, and put
them in a glass bowl.

2. Heat the cream in the top
of a double boiler until it
steams but doesn't bubble.

3. Pour the hot cream over
the broken chocolate and
whisk until evenly blended.
The glaze should be glossy
and smooth. If you get something that looks like speckled
chocolate milk, microwave it
for 10 seconds on high
power and whisk vigorously.
If the problem persists,
microwave it for another 5
seconds and whisk again. It's
better to fix it in small increments of heat than to risk
burning it. (An alternative
solution is to put the cup in 1
inch of simmering water and
whisk until smooth.)

Simple sugars, white and colored, fine-grained and coarse, and sugar decorations are a mainstay of artful cupcakes.

BAKING TIP:
Decorative Sugars

Since sugar decorating is so easy and we love its simple, elegant effect on cupcakes, we use it in many of the projects in the book.

* Sanding sugar comes in many colors. It's mixed with carnuba wax and is coarser than table sugar.

* Coarse sugar is chunky sugar, about four times bigger than sanding sugar.

* Extra-fine sugar, popular in European recipes, is finer ground than table sugar. You can make your own by putting granulated sugar in the blender and grinding it.

* Confectioners' sugar is a finely ground sugar that contains a little cornstarch so it dissolves quickly. This sugar makes wonderful thin coatings for the tops of cupcakes and can also be used as a decorative base on which to display cupcakes.

* Sugar decorations, such as drageé balls and sprinkles, are easy-to-add colorful touches.

Show-Off Cake Vase with Fondant Flowers

Everything in this fantastic cake and cupcake display is edible and delicious, from the sky blue vase to the orange poppy petals. Learn to shape the first few flowers and then making a whole bouquet will be as easy as, well, a vase of cake!

Materials

4 layers of Lemon Poppy Seed Madeira Cake, each 8 inches square (recipe page 131)

2 recipes Classic Buttercream Frosting (recipe page 19)

48 oz (2 recipes) Tasty Fondant (page 130)

Royal Icing (recipe page 65)

12 cupcakes, your choice of flavor

Food coloring in your choice of colors for vase and flowers

Confectioners' sugar

Parchment paper

Toothpicks

Special Tools

Long serrated knife or cake cutter

Marble slab or other smooth surface

Rolling pin

1-inch and 3-inch circular biscuit or cookie cutters

Pastry bags with star tips for each flower color

Instructions: Make the Cake Vase

1. When the four Madeira cakes are cool, use a serrated knife or cake cutter to trim the rounded tops off each one, making them flat.

2. Cut each cake in half horizontally, making eight layers. (See page 14 for cake cutting tips.)

3. Reserve two cake layers. Frost the remaining six layers thinly with the buttercream, just enough to hold them together, and stack them.

4. Using the long serrated knife, start from the top of the stacked layers and slice through them at an angle, making the sides of the vase. Use the photos at left to guide you. Keep the base of the vase at least 6 inches in diameter for stability. Be careful not to remove too much from the sides, as this will make your vase unstable.

Instructions: Decorate the Vase

1. Invert the vase onto a cake board or plate and frost it with a very thin layer of buttercream. This layer holds the fondant on the cake, so it doesn't have to be pretty.

2. Using about a pound of fondant (about a third of the total amount), add a few drops of food coloring in the shade you want the vase to be. Knead the fondant, adding more color if necessary, until the desired hue is reached and the color is uniform throughout.

3. Use a rolling pin to roll out the colored fondant on a smooth surface (such as a marble slab) to a thickness of about ⅛ inch. Use plenty of confectioners' sugar to keep it from sticking. (See the Polka Dot Fondant project on page 20 for some tips on working with fondant.)

127

4. Drape the rolled fondant over the upside-down vase, shaping and smoothing out any wrinkles with your hands.

5. With a paring knife, cut away the excess fondant on the bottom, leaving a 1-inch lip around what will become the top when the cake is inverted.

6. Turn the vase right side up and place it on whatever surface you've chosen as your display plate or area. With your fingers, shape the 1-inch lip around the top (use the project photo to guide you).

7. Make a parchment pastry bag (see instructions on page 101) and fill it with the Royal Icing. Pipe filigree around the top of the vase.

Instructions: Make the Display Tiers inside the Vase

1. With a sharp paring knife, cut one of the reserved cake layers into a 4-inch-diameter disk and the other into a 2-inch-diameter disk. Spread the bottoms of each with the buttercream frosting.

2. Frosting side down, place the larger cake disk on top of the cake that is inside the center of the vase.

3. Set the smaller disk, frosting side down, on top of that one. You now have two tiers on which you can display the flower cupcakes to make them appear as if they're in a mounded bouquet.

Instructions: Make the Cupcake Bouquet

1. Use the serrated knife to slice off the tops of the cooled cupcakes. Frost them with the remaining buttercream, plain or colored as you wish.

2. Make the fondant flowers and let them dry. (See instructions at right.)

3. When all the flowers have dried completely, place them on top of the frosted cupcakes. Arrange the cupcakes

on the tiers on the top of the vase as desired, tilting the bottom layer of cupcakes outward to rest on the lip of the vase for a more rounded effect.

4. Display the remaining cupcakes around the bottom of the vase.

5. Stand back and take a bow.

Design Tip

Three different flowers peek out of the bouquet in the photo, giving it a cheerful, summery look. Similar flowers in different shades of the same color, such as ivory or pink, would give your project a more formal look–something you might like for a fancy wedding or a dinner party.

Make the Flowers

Here are the techniques to make the three different flowers in the photo: the ruffled-petal double-blooming poppies, the radiating petal orange black-eyed Susans, and the simple purple violets.

1. Divide and color the fondant according to what kinds of flowers you plan to put in the bouquet.

• *All poppies*: divide the fondant in half and color one a dark and the other a light shade of the color you prefer. (We used two shades of pink.)
* *All black-eyed Susans*: color the fondant orange or deep yellow.
* *All violets*, color the fondant purple.
* *Three flowers*: divide the fondant into thirds: orange, purple, and pink (then divide in half again for two different shades.)

2. Divide and color the Royal Icing according to the colors of the flower centers.

• *Black* for poppies and black-eyed Susans (Black food coloring can be found in the cake-decorating section of craft stores, or in a specialty baking store.)

• *Yellow* for black-eyed Susans, and violets

• *Red* for poppies

Double-Blooming Poppies

1. Roll the two different shades of fondant out flat to about a ⅛-inch thickness.

2. Use circular cookie cutters or biscuit cutters to cut out two different sizes of petals. First cut out two 3-inch-diameter circles from one shade of the color. Then cut out a single 3-inch-diameter circle from the other shade. From the center of this single circle, cut out a 1-inch circle for the small, narrow petal in the center of the flower.

3. Roll a toothpick around the outside of the circles to ruffle the edges, beginning with one of the two identically colored 3-inch circles. Next do the circle with the hole cut out of the middle. Use a little water to glue this second circle inside the first, keeping the petals separated. Roll the toothpick around the last 3-inch circle and use a little water to nest it inside the second one. Do the

same with the 1-inch circle, leaving a space inside for the center of the flower.

4. Use pastry bags fitted with star tips to pipe the black and red colored Royal Icing to make the centers.

Black-Eyed Susans

1. Make a base for each flower: form a disk of colored fondant about the size of a nickel and set it aside to harden for about an hour.

2. Make the petals for each flower: pinch off a bit of fondant about the size of a nickel and place it on a well-sugared work surface. Roll and press it into a petal shape with your hands. Repeat until you make as many petals as you want, about 15 per flower.

4. With a bit of water, adhere the petals to the hardened fondant base. Adjust the fullness of your petals as desired, then turn the flower upside down, base up, to dry for at least an hour. When the petals are stiff, put the flower right side up.

5. Using the pastry bags fitted with star tips, pipe the colored Royal Icing to make black and yellow centers.

Violets

1. Using purple colored fondant, follow the steps for black-eyed Susans, shaping petals to resemble those of a violet.

2. Pipe in a center with yellow Royal Icing.

Tasty Fondant

Fondant creates a smooth, sleek finish that looks elegant but often tastes less than delicious. This recipe provides a fondant that is flexible to work with, lovely to look at, and yummy on the tongue.

1 egg white

2 tablespoons liquid glucose
(found in pharmacies and on the Internet)

1½ lb confectioners' sugar, sifted, plus more for dusting

Pinch of vegetable shortening

Liquid food coloring

1. Combine the egg white and glucose in a large mixing bowl.

2. Slowly add the confectioners' sugar, stirring with a wooden spoon until a thick paste forms. (The mixture looks like children's sculpting dough but is a little softer.)

3. Turn the mixture out onto a very clean table dusted with confectioners' sugar and knead with your hands until a smooth, silky paste forms.

4. If the mixture begins to dry out or crack while kneading, work in a pinch of vegetable shortening.

5. When the silky consistency is achieved, store the fondant in an airtight container in the refrigerator until you are ready to use. (It will keep up to two weeks.)

6. Allow it to come to room temperature and knead it lightly before using. Again, if it has dried a bit during storage and cracks while kneading, incorporate a little more vegetable shortening.

7. Add liquid food coloring sparingly just before using. Work in a drop at a time while kneading until the desired color is achieved.

Yields 24 ounces or 3 cups
Recipe by Peter Hall

Lemon Poppy Seed Madeira Cake

¾ cup (1½ sticks) unsalted butter,
room temperature

¾ cup of sugar

3 eggs

2 tablespoons poppy seeds

1 tablespoon lemon extract

1 tablespoon vanilla extract

Zest from one lemon

¾ cup self-rising flour

6 tablespoons all-purpose flour

Note: This recipe makes one layer, but you'll need four for the cake in this project. You can increase the recipe four times if you have a very, very large bowl to mix the batter in, but it would be better to double it and make two 8-inch layers twice. If you do make four layers at once, the time it takes to bake may increase some because of the increased humidity in the oven. Begin testing at 45 minutes.

1. Preheat the oven to 375°F and grease and flour an 8-inch cake pan, or prepare a muffin pan for a dozen cupcakes.

2. In a large bowl, cream the butter and sugar until light and fluffy.

3. Add the eggs one at a time until thoroughly combined.

4. Add the poppy seeds, lemon extract, vanilla, and lemon zest.

5. Sift together the self-rising and all-purpose flour, then add.

6. Spoon the thick batter into the pan and bake for approximately 45 minutes for a cake or 15 to 20 minutes for cupcakes, or until a toothpick inserted comes out clean.

Note: In England this cake was traditionally served with madeira wine, thus its name.

Yields one 8-inch layer or 12 cupcakes

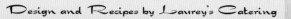

Chocolate Pyramids

It's a pyramid, so naturally there's a secret treasure inside. And this one is tastier than most—a rich filling of chocolate mousse. Another secret is one that makes this project so easy—muffin pans with cups that are already shaped like pyramids. What will they think of next?

Materials

6 Chocolate Pyramid Cupcakes and Base (recipe page 135)

Chocolate Mousse Filling (recipe page 134)

Chocolate Glaze (recipe page 134)

Parchment paper

Special Tools

Wide spatula

Flexible silicone, pyramid-shaped muffin pan

Instructions

1. When the pyramid cakes are completely cooled, use a small paring knife to carefully hollow out the inside of each. Be sure to keep the sides thick enough so the pyramid won't collapse.

2. Reserve the cake you scooped out and set it aside in a bowl for use later.

3. Spoon the Chocolate Mousse Filling into the hollows.

4. Put the cakes back in the baking molds and chill until the mousse is firmly set.

5. While waiting, cut the parchment paper into 6 squares that are about 1 inch wider than the pyramid cakes. Prepare a cooling rack over a clean baking sheet and set the parchment papers nearby.

6. Now you'll make the base for each pyramid, using the completely cooled cake that you baked in the jelly roll pan.

Take each chilled pyramid out of the muffin pan and place it, right side up, one at a time, onto the cake base. Use the paring knife to cut out the cake around the base to fit the pyramid. The pyramids won't be equal in size, which is why you have to individually cut the base for each one.

7. Use the wide spatula to carefully move the pyramids and their bases to a cooling rack placed over parchment paper.

8. Place the excess sheet cake from the pan into the bowl of crumbs you set aside in step 2 and crumble it, too. Sprinkle some of the crumbs onto the four edges of each square of parchment paper, making a crumb perimeter that you'll put the cupcake into later, in step 12.

9. Warm the glaze gently to get it to pouring consistency. It doesn't need to be hot, just liquid.

10. Use a small spoon or ladle to drizzle the warm glaze over each pyramid and its base to create a smooth coating that completely covers it, like paint, which will help hold the two pieces together. (Don't use a spatula or knife to apply the glaze since that would change the surface texture.)

11. Allow the excess glaze to drip into the pan below. If needed, the glaze that has dripped onto the pan can be scraped up with a spatula and reheated to be drizzled again.

12. One at a time, carefully lift each coated pyramid with the wide spatula. Don't touch the sides with your fingers; use your fingers to nudge it along from the bottom. Place it on the crumb-covered parchment paper. Then carefully lift up each edge of the paper so crumbs will gently trickle down to cover each side of the bottom of the cake. Try to make the line as straight as possible, but don't worry if it's a little crooked. Practice makes perfect.

13. Chill each pyramid before serving.

Design Tip

When using the new silicone muffin pans, be sure to follow the manufacturer's instructions in case you need to adjust baking times designed for metal pans. The muffin pans are flexible, so all you have to do is press gently on the bottom of the cup and the cupcake will pop out, its sides smooth.

Chocolate Glaze

4 oz high quality semisweet chocolate (don't use chips)
2 tablespoons heavy cream
2 tablespoons milk
2 tablespoons water
2 teaspoons corn syrup

1. Chop the chocolate into fine pieces.

2. In a saucepan, bring the other ingredients to a boil.

3. Remove the mixture from the heat and add the chocolate pieces. Stir until the chocolate is completely melted. Allow the glaze to cool to room temperature so you can use 4 tablespoons of it to make the Chocolate Mousse Filling. The rest will be used to ice the pyramids.

Chocolate Mousse Filling

8 oz heavy cream
4 tablespoons Chocolate Glaze (recipe above), room temperature

1. Whip the cream to very soft peaks.

2. Add the chocolate glaze, and whip until stiff.

Chocolate Pyramid Cupcakes and Base

14 oz sugar

13 oz flour

2 oz unsweetened cocoa powder

3 teaspoons baking powder

1 teaspoon salt

8 oz (2 sticks) unsalted butter, softened

1 cup milk

4 eggs

1 tablespoon hot water

Special Tools

Silicone muffin pan with pyramid-shaped cups

Jelly roll pan (17¼ X 12¼ inches with a shallow rim) or half-sheet pan

Electric mixer with a paddle attachment

1. Preheat the oven to 325°F. Prepare the muffin pan with nonstick spray. (If you use the silicone coated baking pans in the photo, you don't need to spray them.) Line the jelly roll pan with parchment paper and spray it, too.

2. In the bowl of the electric mixer, using the paddle attachment, blend the dry ingredients and the butter until well blended.

3. Add the milk and eggs and mix thoroughly.

4. Add the hot water. Continue to mix until well blended.

5. Use about half of the batter to fill the cups in the muffin pan approximately two-thirds full.

6. Bake for 15 to 20 minutes, or until a toothpick inserted comes out clean. Remove from the oven and let cool for 5 minutes in the pan, then turn out the cupcakes onto a cooling rack.

7. Turn up the oven temperature to 350°F. Pour the remainder of the batter into the prepared jelly roll pan. When the oven is ready, bake for approximately 8 minutes, until the cake looks done around the edges and the center springs back when lightly touched. Remove the cake and let it cool.

Pansies in Buttercream

The simplicity of the design is what makes it so elegant–a fresh, edible flower resting on a bed of heavenly buttercream. Who said creating artful cupcakes can't be easy?

Materials

24 Easy Yellow Cupcakes
(recipe page 19)

Classic Buttercream Frosting
(recipe page 20)

Food coloring

Fresh flowers, edible and chemical-free

Before You Start

After you pick your flowers, keep them fresh by wrapping them in moist paper towels and refrigerate them until your'e ready to use them.

Instructions

1. Divide the frosting into separate containers. Add food coloring with a toothpick until you reach your desired color.

2. Frost each cupcake generously.

3. Trim the stems from the flowers.

4. Place one or more flowers on top of the cupcakes, depending on your preference and the size of the flowers. Hold each flower firmly but gently, supporting its underside with your fingers and the top with your thumb. Use the photo to guide you.

5. If you wish, decorate the display plate with edible flowers and leaves.

Edible Flowers

If a flower has been sprayed with chemicals at any time during its growth, no matter how edible you might think it is, don't use it to decorate food. Buy only organically grown edible flowers from sources you know and trust. Here are some of the most common edible flowers.

Calendula
Carnations
Cornflowers
Daisies
Fruit flowers such as apple, cherry, lemon, peach, and plum blossoms
Herb flowers such as basil, lavender, mint, and pineapple sage
Impatiens
Leaves of scented geraniums
Lilac
Marigolds
Nasturtiums
Pansies
Roses, including separate rose petals and miniature roses
Squash blossoms
Violas

Note: It's always wise to use only edible flowers and plants in displays of food because guests usually assume that anything on the table near food is edible.

Design and Recipe by Chris Kobler

Raspberry Hearts

You don't need words—these lovely raspberry cupcakes will deliver your sweet message all by themselves. They're as perfect for a candlelit dinner as they are for breakfast in bed.

Materials

Easy Yellow Cupcakes batter, unbaked (recipe page 19)

1 cup seedless raspberry preserves

¼ cup water

½ pint fresh raspberries

4 oz white chocolate

Special Tools

10½ x 15-inch jelly roll pan (looks like a baking sheet with a slightly higher rim to contain thinly spread cake batter)

Heart-shaped cookie cutter(s)

Serrated knife or knife cutter

Pastry brush

Instructions

1. Preheat the oven to 375°F.

2. Prepare the jelly roll pan by lightly oiling it and then pressing waxed or parchment paper over the bottom to fit.

3. Spread prepared Easy Yellow Cupcake batter evenly in the pan and place in the oven to bake.

4. Start checking the cake for doneness after 12 minutes. Look for slight browning at the edges and a dry surface. When a toothpick inserted comes out clean, remove the pan and cool the cake on a wire rack.

5. While the cake is cooling, melt the raspberry preserves with the water in a saucepan over medium heat. Stir it until it's smooth and keep it warm over low heat.

6. When the cake is cool, use heart-shaped cookie cutters to cut out as many hearts as you can. You can use more than one size of cutter, if you like. The number of hearts will vary according to the size(s) of your cutters.

7. If the cake is more than ½ inch thick, use a serrated knife or a knife cutter to split the hearts horizontally to form two layers (see the tips on cutting cakes on page 14).

8. If the cake is ½ inch or thinner, simply stack two hearts without splitting them.

9. Using the pastry brush, spread a layer of the melted jam on one heart cake and top it with another heart. Spread jam on the top heart, too.

10. Arrange fresh raspberries as you like on the top layer—the jam will hold them in place.

11. Glaze the top by painting the berries with a fork dipped into melted jam.

12. Melt the white chocolate. (See Design Tip below for instructions.)

13. Dip a fork into the chocolate and, using the tines of the fork, drip the chocolate delicately across the raspberries. Go in one direction at a time to make thick, luxurious strands.

14. Allow the white chocolate to cool, and serve.

Design Tip

White chocolate "breaks" easily. It is simplest to melt it in a microwave oven in 10-second increments, stirring in between phases just until melted. If you don't have a microwave, a double boiler works well, but just make sure you put the chocolate in a pan *over*, not *in*, warm water.

139

Equivalents and Metric Conversions

More and more cupcake lovers are seeking recipes and decorating tips from around the world, especially on any one of the numerous baking websites on the Internet. Here are some handy charts to help you calculate equivalencies and convert U.S. to metric and vice versa.

WEIGHT EQUIVALENTS

1 cup granulated sugar = 8 oz	
1 cup brown sugar, packed = 6 oz	
1 cup confectioners' sugar = 4½ oz	
1 cup all-purpose flour (unsifted) = 5 oz	
1 cup heavy cream = 2 to 2½ cups whipped	

MEASURING EQUIVALENTS

3 teaspoons = 1 tablespoon	
8 tablespoons = ½ cup	
16 tablespoons = 1 cup	
2 cups = 1 pint	
4 cups = 1 quart	
1 pound = 16 oz	
1 liquid oz = 2 tablespoons	
4 liquid oz = ½ cup	

APPROXIMATE METRIC WEIGHT CONVERSIONS

Ounces (oz) & Pounds	Grams (g)
¼ oz =	7 g
⅓ oz =	10 g
½ oz =	14 g
1 oz =	28 g
2 oz =	57 g
3 oz =	85 g
3½ oz =	100 g
4 oz (¼ pound) =	114 g
8 oz (½ pound =	227 g
16 oz (1 pound) =	554 g

APPROXIMATE METRIC TEMPERATURE CONVERSIONS

F (Fahrenheit)	C (Celsius)
32° (water freezes)	0°
203° (simmer)	95°
212° (boil)	100°
300° oven, slow	150°
350° oven, moderate	180°
400° oven, hot	200°

APPROXIMATE METRIC LIQUID CONVERSIONS

Spoons & Cups	Milliliters (ml) & Liters (L)
1 tsp =	5 ml
2 tsp =	10 ml
3 tsp (1 Tbs) =	15 ml
3⅓ Tbs. =	50 ml
¼ cup =	60 ml
⅓ cup =	80 ml
8 oz (1 cup) =	240 ml
1 cup + ½ Tbs =	¼ L
2 cups + 2½ Tbs =	½ L
4⅓ cups =	1 L

APPROXIMATE METRIC LENGTH CONVERSIONS

Inches & Feet	Centimeters (cm)
1 inch (in) =	2.54 cm
4 inches (in) =	10.2 cm
8 inches (in) =	20.3 cm
12 inches (1 foot) =	30.5 cm
20 inches (in) =	50.8 cm

Contributing Designers

All of our contributing designers live and work in the Asheville, North Carolina, area.

Linda Brown loves chocolate and desserts so much she was inspired to complete the Baking and Pastry Program at Asheville-Buncombe Technical College. She has subsequently finished the school's Culinary Program as well. Linda and her husband Bill dream of opening a bed and breakfast inn where Linda will do the baking and pastries, and Bill will do the gourmet cooking.

Charles deVries creates artistic masterpieces with little more than sugar and chocolate. He credits his French grandmother with sparking his interest in food. A graduate of the Culinary Institute of America and a certified Executive Pastry Chef, Charles has won numerous awards and has participated by invitation in the prestigious Patisfrance Pastry competition in New York City. He and his wife, Telle King, own **Chez Nous Confections**, which specializes in customized wedding and other occasion cakes, chocolate and sugar art, and gourmet chocolate truffles.

www.cheznousconfections. com,cheznous@infionline.net, (828) 658-9919

Veronika Alice Gunter is not a professional baker, but she loves to make treats with all-vegetarian ingredients: dark chocolate cookies, cakes, cupcakes, and muffins. She encourages you to discover vegan recipes on the web and in cookbooks.

Sarah and Pete Hall are chefs at the Mountain Air Country Club in Burnsville. They own **P.S. Customized Cakes** which makes outrageously creative custom-designed cakes, including cupcake wedding cakes. When not cooking or baking, they're playing with their daughter, Addison Louise. Their gingerbread creations will appear in the *Weekend Crafter: Gingerbread Houses* (Lark Books 2004). Pscustomcakes@aol.com, or petehall@hotmail.com, (828) 682-2270

Chris Kobler caters wildly creative meals as a private chef and serves as a consultant to bakeries across the United States. In 1991, he founded the Blue Moon Bakery, and has since started three other bakeries. Besides writing poetry and political speeches, he has authored *Making Great Sausage* (Lark Books, 1999). chriskobler@msn.com

Laurey Masterton is the ace caterpillar-cupcake wizard and proprietor of **Laurey's Catering**, which has operated since 1987. In 1997, Laurey was selected as Small Business of the Year for North Carolina and Small Business Leader of the Year for Asheville. She is the youngest daughter of Elsie and John Masterton, authors of the *Blueberry Hill Cookbooks* and founders of the Blueberry Hill Inn in Goshen, Vermont. www.laureysyum.com, (828) 252-1500

The Sisters McMullen Bakery, owned by **Heather McMullen** and **Andrea McMullen Sailer**, opened its doors in January, 2001. Its menu is influenced by the sisters' shared memories of the baking they did as girls raised in Lancaster, Pennsylvania. Heather, with an Associate in Arts degree in Culinary Arts from Asheville-Buncombe Technical College, has 20+ years' experience in the restaurant industry. Andrea has a Master's degree in Public Administration. thesistersmcmullen@netzero.net (828) 252-9330

Emma Pearson combines her work as an artist with her love of cooking by creating colorful and delicious offerings for the table. She was born in Wales and spent most of her life in the United Kingdom and in Europe. Her artwork is on display at Woolworth Walk in downtown Asheville, and she's created projects for three other Lark Books, *Halloween: A Grown-up's Guide to Creative Costumes, Devilish Decor, and Fabulous*

Festivities (2003), *Gifts for Baby: Toys, Clothes and Nursery Accents to Make with Love* (2003) and *Scarecrows & Yard Figures* (2004). www.pellyfish.com, pellyfish@yahoo.com

Rose Reitzel-Perry began her bakery training at a tender age—her mother started teaching her to bake as soon as she could stand on a stool and reach the counter. Food has always been a central part of her family's life, and Rose now crafts specialty cakes with her sister in a business named **Rose and Lilly's Cakes**. She was 2001 Pastry Student of the Year in the Asheville-Buncombe Technical College Baking and Pastry Arts Program. (828) 236-0234

Avi Sommerville is a self-taught chef, baker, and caterer and owner of **Taste of Heaven Baked Goods**, which sells the world's best carrot cakes online at www.worlds-bestcarrotcake.com. She spends half the year with some of her children at her husband's family homestead in rural Pennsylvania. With its enormous Victorian mansion, the property will become the site of a sustainable living and arts center, offering workshops and retreats as well as an organic farm. avirs444@yahoo.com, (828) 658-0809 or (814) 345-5363

Jane Tomlinson grew up on a peanut farm in Arabi, Georgia, and as a youngster learned to bake her grandmother's Southern Cream Cheese Pound Cake. Years later, it proved extremely popular as the recipe for the wedding cakes she made in her catering business. After deciding that people ought to be able to eat her cake without having to get married, Jane and her husband Don started the **Cakes by Jane** mail-order cake business in 1997. www.cakesbyjane.com, jane@cakesby jane.com, (888) 834-9981

Martha Vining has given more than a thousand cooking and baking demonstrations at the Biltmore Estate Winery. The baking classes she teaches at the John C. Campbell Folk School in Brasstown, North Carolina, are always filled to capacity. She has baked at restaurants in Chicago, Boston, and London. A graduate of the Cordon Bleu Cooking School in London, she has also written feature articles about food for newspapers, Emerils.com, and *National Geographic Traveler*. vining@worldnet.att.net

Mark Zink is the chief spider-cupcake rustler and Executive Pastry Chef at **Laurey's Catering**. He previously worked in the same capacity at The Water Club in Manhattan, and Commander's Palace and Bayona in New Orleans. www.laureysyum.com, (828) 252-1500

Marcianne Miller is the author of several Lark Books, including *Decorating with Mini-Lights* (2002), *The Ultimate Gel Candle Book* (2002), *Salvage Style for the Garden* (2003), *Silk Flower Arranging: Easy, Elegant Designs* (2003), and *Scarecrows & Yard Figures* (2004). She came to book writing via previous careers in broadcasting and archaeology. She and all the members of her family are devoted cupcake lovers.

143

Acknowledgments

Thank you to all the sweet people whose talent and generosity made this book possible...

Art director Susan McBride
Photographer Sandra Stambaugh

All the creative cupcake bakers who put their hearts into our cupcakes

Our extended Lark Books team:

Megan Kirby, whose idea it was
Vice President, Publishing Director Carol Taylor
Executive Editor, Deborah Morgenthal
Cover Designer Barbara Zaretsky
Assistant Editor Nathalie Mornu
Editorial Interns Robin Heimer and Rebecca Lim
Associate Art Director Shannon Yokeley
Art Intern Avery Johnson
Studio Assistants Delores Gosnell and Anne Hollyfield
Location Coordinator Jeff Hamilton
Proofreader Jeanée M. LeDoux

For the use of their lovely china and vintage linens:
Elisabeth Cauley Bennett, Edna M. Kahl, and Merry Miller

Tex Harrison, owner of Complements to the Chef, for her generous use of props and equipment: 800-895-2433, 828-258-0558, www.complementstothechef.com

For being Cupcake Queens of the Fluffiest Order and working so hard on so many different aspects of the book:
Zoe Evermont, Bunny Feathers, and Sadie Greene

Index

A Note About Suppliers

Usually, the supplies you need for making the projects in Lark books can be found at your local craft supply store, discount mart, home improvement center, retail shop or food market relevant to the topic of the book. Occasionally, however, you may need to buy materials or tools from specialty suppliers. In order to provide you with the most up-to-date information, we have created suppliers listings on our Web site, which we update on a regular basis. Visit us at www.larkbooks.com, click on "Craft Supply Sources," and then click on the relevant topic, such as "Food & Cooking." You'll find numerous companies listed with their web address and/or mailing address and phone number.